Go in Peace

Go in Peace

A Biblical Perspective on Healing for Women

Ruthann Williams, OP

BOOKS & MEDIA

BOSTON

Library of Congress Cataloging-in-Publication Data

Williams, Ruthann.
   Go in peace : a biblical perspective on healing for women /
Ruthann Williams.
      p. cm.
   Originally published: Caldwell, NJ : Sacred Heart Press, c1990.
   ISBN 0-8198-3083-6
   1. Women in the Bible. 2. Women—Religious life. Spiritual
healing. I. Title.
[BS575.W575   1996]
220.9'2'082—dc20   96-9142
                                                              CIP

Cover design: Helen Rita Lane, FSP

http:www.pauline.org
E-mail: PBM_EDIT@INTERRAMP.COM

Printed and published in the U.S.A. by Pauline Books & Media, 50
St. Paul's Avenue, Boston, MA 02130.

Pauline Books & Media is the publishing house of the Daughters of
St. Paul, an international congregation of women religious serving
the Church with the communications media.

1 2 3 4   99 98 97

for the women
who have shaped my life

and the men

and always and ever for
Jesus

Contents

Introduction

My Own Story: An Ordinary Woman

The purpose of my story is not just to tell you about myself, but to share with you my experience of what it means to be a woman. For in the course of my ministry to women, I have discovered that my story is not only mine, but ours. It is the story of an ordinary woman, which is what gives it value. I am just an ordinary woman...who has been touched and blessed and healed. I recount it here for two reasons.

The first is to assure you that you are not alone in your experiences. Many of us—though we might never have admitted it—have walked or run or crawled or flown through each other's dreams and nightmares. All women know this terrain. You are not alone.

My second reason is to give witness that no matter how deep the wound is, Jesus heals! He heals the hemorrhages of our emotional wounds, the scars and scabs of our tortured souls. He restores life when people, ourselves included, have given us up for dead.

God's dream for us has always been that we should become whole and graced human beings. You can be healed and you will be healed if you place yourself totally in God's care.

How can I be so certain? I am certain because I am sitting here on this golden spring day with the sunshine pouring in my windows. I can rejoice in the springtime and the sunlight. I am certain because I have known the darkness and the cold and the ice and the death.

I was the oldest in a family of six children. I was born during a time when the world was fighting a terrible war. I grew up under the shadow of the mushroom clouds of Hiroshima and Nagasaki.

During my childhood my family roamed the country. We moved like gypsies. By the time I was nine we had lived in Connecticut, Illinois, California, Nebraska, Arizona, Nebraska again, and Tennessee. Nor did living in a particular state or even a particular city mean stability. I recall at least four different houses in Nebraska and two in Arizona. Prior to our time in Nebraska I was simply too young to remember things clearly, though I seem to recall at least two or three different apartments in Chicago. In Nashville where I lived for nine years (except for a six-month sojourn to Colorado and two stints in boarding schools), I can count nine different residences. I can't count the schools for certain, however, because sometimes even though our house remained the same, I changed schools. At other times, though the school stayed the same, we changed houses. Why? I honestly don't know.

Though in some respects the gypsy life was exciting, it wounded me. I built "no trespassing" walls around myself because I knew there would come a time when I would have to say good-bye. I learned early that it was much easier to say good-bye if I never really said hello. So the compassionate side of me became frozen, beyond the reach of any human person.

Now I know, though in my denial I didn't realize it until recently, that I am from what is popularly termed a "dysfunctional" family. That puts me in the company of what the experts say is 96% of humanity. The rootlessness alone would have qualified us. But I must add to that a father who was a workaholic and a modestly famous personality which, while it has its advantages, has distinct disadvantages as well; a mother who had experienced great emotional wounding herself as a child; and a sister who was chronically ill with asthma.

I also experienced wonderful things in my childhood. I don't wish to give the impression that it was totally unhappy. My parents loved me and encouraged me to develop my talents, unusual though they might have seemed. In many ways I was spoiled. We all were. My mother used to laugh and say she was probably unique in all the world in that she had "six only children." I had a wonderful, if somewhat roving, education. At a young age I acquired a love of books, good painting, the ballet and the opera. These loves have lasted through my life and have sustained me in times of grief and pain.

But sorrow also invaded my life. When I was four years old, the father of one of my playmates raped me. Then I was hit and run over by a car. This resulted in a very long hospital stay, an even longer recuperation period. It also marked my leg with a permanent scar, which was quite large and ugly. When I was in the fourth grade, a school janitor molested me. In the fifth grade, a thousand or so miles away from the earlier incident, another school employee molested me again.

By the time I was ten I had accepted the blame for all this and thought I was guilty of seduction, even though I wasn't quite sure what that meant. Despite my age at the time of these sexual crimes, I believed myself to be the guilty party. After all, I was the one in control, or so I had been taught and would be taught for several more years, taught by women who were themselves victims of this kind of thinking.

Along with many women my age I grew up believing that the single most important attribute a woman could have was physical beauty. Brains were all right, though never to be flaunted in front of men, but beauty was infinitely better. My younger sister was and is beautiful and she was touted as such throughout her childhood. On the other hand, I was led to believe that I was rather plain, especially in comparison to her. Regardless of the truth, whether I am actually plain or beautiful or somewhere in the middle, I believed myself to be very plain. In my world that was almost a mortal wound. How could I possibly hope to be rescued by the handsome prince (which, of course, was central to a maiden's dream) if I were one of the ugly step-sisters? I don't use the fairytale example lightly. In my childhood "pretty" meant "good." Only the beautiful one got the fairy godmother, went to the ball, and married the prince.

At eighteen and only one year out of high school, I married to prove to my parents just how grown-up I was. I endured that marriage for seven years, and I won't spell out the details. Suffice to say that it was not a marriage made in heaven. When we finally divorced, I blamed my-self and accepted the guilt.

At eighteen I also declared my independence from God, the Church, and all those things that I thought only "weak" people needed. Except for friends' weddings and an occasional funeral, I didn't go back to church for almost twenty years.

I met a man and fell in love, but steadfastly refused to get married. It was the late sixties and I was in my glory, marching against the war and wearing flowers in my hair, careless, carefree and completely removed from my own reality. The life I led was not a holy one, and I am not proud of it. I had learned early that sex was power, perhaps the only power a woman had, and I used it as such. The years passed.

My womanhood was wounded, deeply wounded by others and by myself (not to mention the wounds I had inflicted on others). But if you had asked me, I would have laughed. Me, wounded? No way. I know what being a woman is all about. Haven't I turned my life into a success story, put myself through college and graduate school, put aside flower power and adapted to the "real" world of work? Haven't I molded myself into a new career image? Don't I have a beautiful apartment, sterling and good china for my table, and a mink coat in my closet? Haven't I got a thriving business? Don't I fly first class? Isn't my handsome gentleman caller just what every girl needs to complete her list of possessions? Am I not free, totally free?

The answer was no, though I didn't realize it then. Far from being free, I was bound and gagged by the world, my co-dependent relationship, my isolation from the rest of humanity, my unremitting selfishness and my self-hatred.

In 1975 my father died. If there had been any part of me still open to others, it closed. With the death of my beloved daddy, the only absolute and complete human love I believed I had ever known vanished. There was no one left to call me "Princess," no one who would love me just because I was and not for anything that I could do. Furious at the "fates" that had taken him, I became even more absorbed in protecting myself with money and possessions.

Thank God, and I do thank God every day of my life, that he continued to love me in my woundedness and my delusion. Thank God for caring about what happened to one poor lost woman. Thank God for breaking into my crippled self without my ever consciously asking. Thank God for my healing which continues even into this moment.

God caught me one night over sixteen years ago, as I stood on my back porch, off-guard and unaware, drinking in the April darkness. I had just landed a big client. I had just said goodnight to my friend. I had the world by the tail. Suddenly I thought, _is this all there is?_

The answer God gave me is obvious because here I am: without an apartment, without sterling, without mink, and certainly without gentleman callers. I can tell you that I have never been so happy before, because now I have all there is. Or "All There Is" has me, which is much more to the point.

God has healed me of so many things: of never saying hello and of feeling guilty about being a woman, of defining myself only by the men in my life and of believing that sex is a weapon, of buying into the mistaken notion that other women are my natural enemies and of thinking that what I do is more important than who I am. He has cured me from thinking that my "original sin" is being a woman and has taught me that my womanhood is a gift and a treasure. Much of that teaching has come through my prayer, my life in a community of women, my study of Scripture, and my discovery of all the ways in which our God has blessed and healed women throughout the ages. That is what led me to start days of healing for women. That, in turn, is what led me to write this book—Jesus...and you.

I finally realized that God was, is, and will be there no matter what. When good things happen, it is easy to sense his presence. But even more I've come to understand that when evil occurs he is no less there. This was harder to accept.

For years I struggled with that, wondering why God had made it necessary for me to suffer sexual violence when I was only a small child. Why didn't God stop it? Why didn't he take care of me?

It was only in prayer that I found the answer. God was there. I believe that with all my heart. He was there in all the power of his Spirit, begging the man to stop, but unable to stop him by force lest the gift of free will become an empty joke. I believe with all my heart, too, that God was there with me, weeping at the violence and trying to comfort and sustain me through it all.

Why did it have to happen? Quite simply because the enemy of our souls lives and sometimes people will pay more attention to that enemy than they will to the wonderful truth and goodness of God.

Further, I know that God can and will bring good out of even the most dreadful situations *if we let him.*

God did bring good out of my own suffering. How? Through my ministry to women, which has resulted in this book. When I first began giving days of healing for women and I told my story, I discovered that—without exception—afterward one or two or three or even more women would come up to me and say, "Sister, I never told anyone about this but when I was small...." Then they would relate some incident of sexual abuse. They would say, "I've never been able to forgive myself. I've always felt guilty about it. But now I think maybe there's hope." I pray with them and I continue to pray for them because I know that our God heals all wounds, even the oldest and scabbiest. God has brought good out of my experience. I thank him for that each day. He showed me a path to compassion, which has brought healing to me and through me to others.

I'm certain that each of you, too, has a healing story of your own, ways in which the Lord has touched you and set you free. Do thank him for those graces and, above all, keep your eyes on him as you continue your healing journey in his power and protection.

What he has done for me, he will do for you, I promise. Our healings may be alike or different. But they are all one, because they are really the healings of our gracious God, who loves us so much that he always reaches out to heal us. Open your heart to that love, to that incredibly tender love and find your womanhood embraced and exalted in ways you might never even have imagined.

I leave you now to God and to my labor of love. Know that I am praying with and for you as you continue your healing journey, safe in the arms of Jesus.

Go in peace.

Chapter One

Eve

Guilty...or Innocent?

To begin at the beginning, let's consider Eve, the very first woman of whom we are aware. We all know the story; we practically imbibed it with our mother's milk. Later we were taught it in school by people who meant well, but who were also heirs and heiresses to the tradition.

Put succinctly, we have learned to focus on Eve with the apple, completely overlooking Eve before the apple and Eve after the apple. We have concentrated on the sin, the sinner, the woman. So we grow up daughters of Eve, guilty of the original sin of being women. Not only our activity but our very being is somehow tainted. We are responsible for all the sin and suffering the human race has endured since Eden.

But we all know that, so there is no point in dwelling on it. In fact, let's not even consider it for now. Instead, let's look at Eve from another point of view altogether.

Eve was not created bad, anymore than Adam was created bad. In fact, Eve was one of God's masterpieces.

Look at woman. For just a moment, step back from all preconceptions, all prejudices, all expectations. Simply look at woman. Look at the female body and you will see something very lovely, something very beautiful, something with soft rounded edges and curves, something formed to give and nourish life.

Let us think of ourselves as chalices to be filled with the holy. We are cups. We are potential for new life. We are all kinds of wonderful and sacred things, just as Eve was. But we forget about that too often.

We forget about Eve before the fall, the Eve that God designed in order to complete his creation, the Eve who laughed and ran through the garden and rejoiced in its beauty and maybe even made flower chains for her hair. Eve may even have begun life as a child. We don't know for certain. But if I had to take bets, I'd say so.

Eve was innocent, absolutely innocent and pure and clean and beautiful to behold. That's how woman was created, just as man was created innocent and pure and clean and beautiful to behold.

Eve was good. We must realize that, if we are to reclaim woman as God created her, ourselves as God created us to be. We were not created evil. We were created to be good. We were created to complete God's creation, to bring to it all the things we are, all the things that were lacking before us, all the womanly female feminine things creation needed and still needs to be whole.

The Feminine

Unfortunately, history has convinced us that the feminine is to be equated not only with temptation, but also with passivity, with too much feeling and not enough intellect. To be feminine is to be passionate and emotional, to be capricious and messy and just not quite clean and sharp enough. All of these qualities have come to be considered very negative. They can be, but they are not so by definition. In fact, these feminine attributes, far from being detrimental, are great and incredible blessings from the God who looked on *all* he had made, women included, and pronounced it "very good" (Gen 1:31).

Nor are these attributes all there is to being a woman. We are many other things as well: nurturing, life-bearing, generous. No one would deny us those identities. But what about the rest, those things the "masculine" has claimed for itself? What about courageous and gallant and loyal and wise and thoughtful and prudent? We are those things as well. For the God who created all of us is an inclusive God, a God of the both/and, not the either/or.

But the emphasis in this chapter and, indeed, the entire book is primarily—though not exclusively—on the qualities *labeled* feminine because they have also been *libeled* feminine. Let us renounce the libel and rejoice in the label because feminine is what we are called to be in God's plan for the earth.

Life-Bearers

Life-bearers and life-givers, that is our great calling as women, a call that Eve answered repeatedly both in spirit and in fact. She was named Eve because she was "mother of all the living" (Gen 3:20). As woman she brought to her own children and to all subsequent generations the gift of herself as mother.

What does it mean to be a mother? To a child a mother is feeder, nurturer, clother, comforter, teacher, fount of wisdom and dispenser of all that is necessary for life. She is a hand rocking a cradle, giving a treat; a voice to banish monsters and fears on a dark night; a heart to rejoice in the laughter of her child; a warm and soft bosom, a welcoming lap. As a woman Eve brought these gifts to Cain, to Abel, to Seth, to her "other sons and daughters" (Gen 5:4), and through them and the generations that followed, to us. Eve. Woman. She was the first woman and so the first to give flesh to all that motherhood means.

So too are we called to be mothers. Our very bodily construction is meant to bear and nourish life. Though not all of us have children, does that mean we cannot be life-bearers and life-givers? Does it mean we cannot be mothers? Does it mean we have denied our deepest selves? Not at all. We can find the potential for creating life in whatever situation we find ourselves. That is obedience, just the opposite of the "original sin."

God makes no secret of what his will is for us. In Deuteronomy he makes it quite clear. "I have set before you life and death, blessings and curses. Choose life so that you and your descendants may live, loving the Lord your God, obeying him, and holding fast to him" (Deut 30:19-20). God's will for us is to be mothers, as Eve was mother before us.

Choose life. Who better to choose life than woman who was made for that purpose? How do we choose life? We choose it in a thousand ways. Every day we pass through countless moments in which we make decisions, choices.

Some of them are obviously less important than others. Choosing which soft drink brand to buy is not a momentous decision. But even our supermarket choices can become important once we have decided to become socially conscious, to become "mothers" to social change.

Which companies are not doing justice in their corporate decisions? Which profit from the ill-paid labor of the poor, especially the foreign poor? Which participate in the economies of countries where racial injustice is the law, where human rights are limited to the rich? Which fatten their wallets in nuclear stockpiling? Perhaps there is no such thing as an unimportant choice.

How do we behave at the wheel of a car? Are we life-givers? Or will we take chances, terrify other drivers, put pedestrians in danger in order to get ahead of someone who seems just a little pokey? How do we behave with others in our work places? Are we life-bearers? Or do we kill reputations and hopes and dreams with gossip and jealousy? How do we behave with our spouses, our children, our significant others? What face do we show in our most casual encounters, to the toll collector, the letter carrier, the drugstore clerk, all those people whom we touch each day?

We constantly choose our responses so we need to ask ourselves if we respond as life-givers or do we react as life-takers? Our creation as women enables us to respond in deep and life-giving ways. Our call to be mothers demands that we be about nurturing a "new earth." The choice is ours.

Passion

Is there any woman who has not been "accused" of being too passionate, too emotional? Probably not. We are passionate creatures, and certainly the world could use a bit more real passion, a bit less of the cerebral.

The world would have us intellectualize everything, give all to our brains, and let all behavior be controlled by logic. Of course, we must remember that logic in itself is

not evil. It is part of our human nature. But anything out
of balance is not good. We must remember that this "logical" worldview has been carefully constructed, especially
since the "Age of Reason." The world has come to worship
the rational, the thought-out, the logical. So we move our
feelings into our brains and freeze them there.

You see, brains are safe containers for feelings because brains make everything sharp and hard-edged, a
condition we can deal with. Passion makes people nervous
because it's messy, a condition we don't care to deal with.

God created passion and gave it to us. Jesus felt passion, love, terror, anguish, pain and anger. Because he felt
it, we have been redeemed. A God who insisted on mind
over matter, so to speak, would never have done something so passionate as sending his Son to be one of us. We
need our passions. We need to be in touch with them.
They are part of our holiness.

Women, be passionate as God created you to be
passionate. Will we be mocked? Probably. Will we be ridiculed? More than likely. So was Jesus. But in the end those
passions will be as true to us as they were to him. Though
we may have to endure crucifixion, those passions will also
get us out of the tomb and on to resurrection, for ourselves and for the world.

Compassionate People

In giving us these passions, God gave us a great gift,
for he enabled us to be com-passioned as well. What does
compassion mean? Is it sentimentality? No, though
women are very often labeled "sentimental" when compassionate is a more accurate word.

What does it mean to be compassionate? It means to
feel passion with. It means that we are able to feel with

each other, to understand one another's feeling, and to be willing to work together to make things better or to celebrate when all is well.

Women are very good at celebration. Who usually decides to give parties? We do. We love parties. We love to entertain, to be hostesses, which is one of the largest portions of compassion. Hostessing is God-like. Think of the Eucharist at which God is at once both host of the banquet and the banquet Host. What greater celebration is there, what more compassionate action on the part of our God, than the celebration of that sacred meal?

Most of us, if we think of compassion at all, think of it in its more somber sense. We think of the poor, the ill, the homeless, the hungry. We think of the misery and we miss the deeper point. True compassion leads us to re-creation of this world in the way God has ordained it. True compassion does not dwell on the misery but works to alleviate it so that all may join in the wonderful celebration of life. Who better to "compassion" into life than woman with her passions and her birthing potential?

Playfulness

When the "new heavens and the new earth" that we are promised in Revelation 21 come to pass and there is "no more death or mourning, wailing or pain," perhaps this new creation will be characterized in large part by a great sense of wonder which, I believe, will lead us into play. Play is another of those God-like activities that seems to have fallen into disrepute for everyone much past the age of seven, the age—heaven help us!—of "reason."

But play is a gift we women have, lengthened and strengthened by our relationships with children. Play makes us joyful. Play releases us from too much seriousness.

A friend once said to me that I don't seem to be a very serious person. At first I was highly insulted, only proving that I, too, need all the healing God will give me. But insulted, I was. Here I am, middle-aged, hard working, intelligent, and she thinks I'm not serious? Humph!

Then I began to think about it, probably when I was building a sandcastle or swinging in the park. She was right. Hurrah! I refuse to take life too seriously. I have toys and I play with them...and with children...and with adults when I can find adults who will play with me.

And I play with God who is certainly the best player of all. Who but someone with a fantastic sense of playfulness would have created giraffes or cactus or Spanish moss or snow? Who else would have dreamed of creating people out of mud? Who else would have thought to cure the blind by spitting in their eyes?

Let's join in the play. Let's play at the beach and in the snow, even when it means sand in our swimsuits and snow down our necks. Let's engage ourselves completely in this game with God that we call life and exult in the fact that everyone can win!

Play. We women can do that. I think it makes God laugh when he sees us enjoying this huge playground that he made. Have you ever looked at the world that way, as one huge playground?

Try it. I think Eve did. Take advantage of your feminine gift of play, a gift to cherish and develop and enjoy and embrace, a gift for life.

Another gift for life and play that we have is our intuition. It's a great gift. When we speak of intuition, we're not talking about knowing who's on the other end of the phone when it rings. No, there is a much more important kind of intuition, the intuition which envisions possibilities.

We are visionaries by sex. We're not held back by practicalities, though we know it's a dreadful sin to be impractical. But if we were never impractical, if we never dared to intuit what might be possible, if we never jumped fearlessly into imagination, we'd most likely still be living in caves.

Just between us, I think it was a woman who first discovered fire, a woman who invented the wheel, a woman who first spoke (never mind the jokes that could engender!), and surely a woman who first wrote a poem. All those great leaps of imagination, the what-ifs, the daring to try, even if sometimes too heedless of consequences—those are things that women do.

No, not all consequences are good. The "what-if" is probably what got Eve to bite that apple to begin with. But the gift is good. It is what we do with it that decides if we are choosing life or death, the blessing or the curse. If we bring our best selves to our intuitions, if we invite the holy to come and live in our chalices, we can begin more and more to trust our what-ifs and to act on our imaginings. It is part of our playfulness. It will help to bring about "the new earth."

Someone once referred to women as "terribly capricious." Note the adverb "terribly," not "wonderfully." It was meant as a most unflattering comment. But think about it. Is "capricious" really so terrible? Isn't it perhaps wonderful?

The dictionary calls it "fickle," but what about flexible, free, yielding, open to the Spirit who, like the wind, joyfully blows where it wills instead? (cf. Jn 3:8). Indeed, one book says that the capricious person is guided by a host of things, but never by reason, and operates independently of serious considerations. Sounds good to me!

Consider a world that is a bit less serious, a bit more

capricious, a world that considers play and laughter and singing and writing poems at least as important as military security and boundary setting and governmental systems. As women we are greatly blessed with this capriciousness because it is much easier for us as adults to play and sing and dance and sit on the floor with jacks and a little rubber ball than it is for our adult brothers.

Now call your intuition into play, literally and figuratively, and imagine our world as a place where painting and flowers and playing and hummingbirds are at least as important as making money. Imagine that world and then invite your capricious self to begin to make it happen. A new earth? Oh, yes, and yes again.

Be a Woman

We are passionate and compassionate and life-bearing and creative and capricious and playful. We are all those things because we are women, daughters of Eve, heiresses at least as much to the gifts as to the sin. We can choose which we want to accept: the blessing or the curse, life or death.

This is what it can mean to be a woman and this is what we can celebrate when we hear or read about Eve. The negative things are not good, not holy. Anything or anyone which tells you that woman is lesser is not holy. Don't let it into your sacred vessel. Reject it, and in its place invite the Holy Spirit.

Jesus sent the Spirit to us to fill us with the graces of all our potential, all our goodness, all our possibilities. In that Spirit we are free to embrace who we are and then go on to become all that God has dreamed for us since he first created woman, the creature that he needed to make his work complete.

The Healing

There is great healing for us in this. For though we as women have been more or less liberated, economically and socially, we must be liberated spiritually if liberation is to have any meaning for us. God created Eve. God created us. God intended that we should be free, not chained by past misconceptions of who or what we are, not enslaved by stereotypes, not bound up in history.

No, God created us to be free, free to complete the circle he had designed, to make it whole and life-bearing, intuitive, playful, nurturing—all those gifts that women bring to the rest of creation.

Yes, God created us. There is much healing just in realizing that, that we are created deliberately. We are chosen. We are designed. We're not an accident. We are separate, distinct. If we can, with God's grace, learn to embrace and become that, we will find the liberation we most need: the salvation of our womanhood.

Prayer

Gracious God, I have called on you in this moment to thank you for myself. I thank you for having made me a woman and for having given me the gifts and talents which you did. I thank you for choosing to give me life and for enabling me to give life to others. I thank you that laughter is easy for me. I thank you that I like to play. I thank you for this playground earth which you have strewn lavishly with beautiful and wonderful things.

I ask you to liberate me into myself, to help me discover all the things of which I am capable, and all the ways of being which can be mine in you. I want your vision, God, so that I can imagine your hope for the future. I want to be what you created me to be: a woman who has a necessary place in your creation. I want to be that woman as fully and completely as I can.

Thank you for all the graces of my life, including the grace which I experience now: your call to me to come to you and to discover in your embrace how "very good" I am.

Mother Eve, pray for me and for all your daughters. Amen.

Chapter Two

Vashti and Company
The High Cost of Being Beautiful

To be beautiful is at once a blessing and a curse. The blessing is an obvious one, or so it would seem. But as so many beautiful women have said, often the curse isn't so apparent to those of us who are more ordinary in appearance. The curse is that people rarely see anything about a beautiful woman except her beauty. That's another kind of enslavement.

But what is beauty all about? Is it merely decorative, a nonessential grace strewn randomly around the female— and the male—population?

A poet once wrote that "if eyes were made for seeing, then beauty is its own excuse for being." It's a lovely thought, but perhaps it doesn't reflect the most Godly perspective. Everything we have and are is in service to God and to his plan for us. If we are to find the true service of the blessing in beauty, we must pray for the Spirit's gifts of wisdom and understanding.

Beauty is a gift. We cannot earn it. We are born that way or another. Honestly, it seems that it is a gift which

God has distributed rather more generously than not. Women are beautiful creatures, by and large. We are shaped in soft and rounded ways. Our features are delicate and gently shaded. Generally speaking, our bones are finer and our wrists are smaller than those of our brothers. Our feminine beauty is God's gift to us. We need to be grateful for it as for any gift. Most often lacking the physical strength of men, we have nonetheless been given beauty which has a strength of its own, a strength intended to be used for the kingdom of God.

How? Why? Popular culture tells us that beauty, enhanced or produced by an endless assortment of products and/or surgeries, is necessary for happiness. And how do we find happiness? In sexy clothes, sexy cars, sexy sound systems, sexy food, sexy sex. Our culture tells us that beauty is necessary for happiness and happiness is sex— not love, but sex.

Please, understand that I am not opposed to sex. It is another mighty gift from God and as such it can and should be holy. A man and a woman, bound in spousal love by the Holy Spirit, find in the sexual expression of that love great delight. That also is part of what God called "very good" when he looked at all he had made.

But commercialized sex, the kind which trivializes and even denies our holiness, has nothing to do with a graced gift. It is very far from what God had in mind.

Setting that aside, then, what is the true use of beauty? What place does it have in God's plan for our salvation? Once more we turn to the Old Testament. Immediately four names come to mind: Vashti, Esther, Susannah and Bathsheba. In the stories of these women we can find models and warning and at least some of God's reasons for having made women beautiful.

Vashti

Except for Scripture scholars and a few other individuals, probably not very many people are familiar with Vashti. I only found her by accident when I was busily looking through the book of Esther to be certain I had my facts straight about her. Quite unexpectedly, I found a heroine! For the wounded women that we are, Vashti is a woman to be admired. She appears and disappears very quickly. But in a short space she tells a sad and proud story.

Vashti was a queen, married to King Ahasuerus "who ruled over one hundred twenty-seven provinces from India to Ethiopia" (Esth 1:1). In the garden court of the palace, the king gave a party which lasted for seven days. It goes without saying that the king and his male guests were a bit worse for wear as he had ordered that the drinking be "unstinted" (Esth 1:8). The queen also gave a party, though Scripture doesn't say whether or not the ladies gave in quite so freely to the spirit of the grape.

Being "merry with wine" (Esth 1:10), Ahasuerus ordered that Vashti be sent in to his party so that he could show off her beauty to everyone. Just for a moment, imagine yourself in Vashti's place. This was no loving request, no cherishing desire, no command that showed any respect for her person, her virtue or her intellect. This was a drunken order that she come and exhibit herself like some sort of object to a group of drunks. We know what would have been on their minds, and it wasn't a regard for her value as a human person.

Vashti said "no." I might as well tell you now as later that her courage was not rewarded in this life. She was banished and soon replaced. Such was the power of the king. But for a moment let's look at the power of Vashti.

Her "no" was much greater than just an act of defiance. It was taking a stance for beauty as something more than "its own excuse for being." Vashti refused to be "objectified." She stalwartly took her stand and chose banishment over slavery. Slavery is just that: becoming someone else's object.

What a joyful message she leaves for us. We need not and must not allow ourselves to be depersonalized. That is not what beauty is all about. If we believe that no part of Scripture is there by accident, then we have God's message. Vashti's tragic and heroic story is meant for us to hear and learn from.

Why say it is a joyful message when the denouement is so unhappy? Because, my sisters, she was braver than we may ever have to be, "kings" being not quite so powerful now as then. Of course, we can be divorced, ignored, neglected, ridiculed, accused of being unfeminine, or made the butt of unkind remarks. But we can't be banished. We can stay and stand and live *in* the face of it all and *for* the beautiful faces of all. If Vashti were so brave, so insistent on her personhood, can we be any less?

Yet time after time, we do allow ourselves to be treated as something not quite human. We allow ourselves to be made into objects. We bow meekly to the terrible command, explicitly or implicitly made, and we become *things,* albeit beautiful things.

Worse, we do it to each other. We congratulate little girls not on being brave or bright, but on being pretty. We look with envy and often with dislike on beautiful women. We bow to the dictates of the cosmetic and fashion monarchs and do all in our power to be...what? Objects of beauty? Then beware, for we have objectified ourselves. Once we accept that mindset we are on a path to disaster.

Sadly, objectification has taken over much of our worldview. It has set up an unhealthy dichotomy that, unchecked, means not only the degradation of people, of peoples, but also of the whole of creation. The objectification of human beauty is symptomatic of a disease which has gripped us and which ultimately could destroy us.

Objectification says, "I, me, mine"; it claims "my life, my wants, my comfort, my food, my desires, mine, mine, mine," without thought for the price others will have to pay for "my" satisfaction. Ahasuerus said, "my possession," without regard to Vashti's personhood. And we, especially in this century, have said, "my earth," and so make it an object separate from ourselves to be exploited.

Vashti knew the dangers of objectification. We must claim her vision quickly and realize that objectification has caused women...and men...and children...and the planet...and the entire cosmos to be profaned. For if we are capable of stripping people of their humanity, how very easy it becomes to strip our forests and seas and animals and even the air we breathe of their holiness, their necessary part in God's plan.

Nothing is "mine." Nothing is even "ours." All is God's: the universe, this planet, men, women, children. When we forget that for even the briefest instant, we are in danger.

What has been and is being done to women, with and without our unfortunate cooperation, is being and has been done to the earth. Rape, defilement and degradation are the awful words which describe how we have abused the beauty of this planet. Because it is there and helpless, we have made it an object, have polluted the air and the water, have denuded the forests, have used concrete instead of compassion in our striving to gain "mastery" over this home of ours.

But because we are beautiful and because we know what subjugation and degradation are like, God is gracing

us to be able to resonate with the passion of this planet
and to use our gifts of compassion and celebration and
beauty to save it.

Nothing is an accident. So we find in our double gifts
of beauty and compassion a cosmic challenge to bring the
earth back to wholeness, to help it to heal. We, who know
what it is like to be mistreated with impunity, can more
clearly understand what is being done to the earth. And,
as Vashti, we can defy—in the power of beauty—those
who would continue to destroy God's creation.

Esther

Beauty can also be used to create justice. We need
only read through the rest of the book of Esther to discover that.

Esther was Vashti's successor as Queen of Persia. She
was a Jewess, unbeknown to the king. Because Esther's
uncle refused to pay sufficient obeisance to the vizier of
the king, the king was cajoled into promulgating a decree
which authorized the slaughter of all the Jews in the kingdom. When Esther learned of this, she went to the king to
plead the cause of the Jewish people.

It all sounds rather simple, but in fact it was a danger-
ous thing for Esther to do for a number of reasons. First, it
meant identifying herself as a Jewess. Even more, it meant
disobeying the law that forbade anyone to approach the
king in his inner court unless that person was summoned.
The punishment for disobedience was death.

Esther spent three days in prayer and fasting before
she went to the king. In preparing herself, she made full
use of the gift of her beauty. She "arrayed herself in
splendid attire.... She was radiant with perfect beauty, and
she looked happy" (Esth D:2-5).

Despite the law and despite her "civil disobedience," Esther succeeded in turning aside the wrath of the king from herself and from her people. Beauty triumphed. So did life-giving. Although Esther's plan resulted in the death of the evil vizier, it was not at her request or desire. She only asked that her uncle's service to the king be recognized and that the king remit the punishment he had decreed for her people. She made no request for power for herself. She did not demand the death of her enemy.

Because of Esther's holy use of her beauty, she saved her people and justice was done. What a contrast that is to the selfish use of beauty. Of course, the whole story is a bit more detailed than what is related here. But one thrust of Esther is this: beauty is given for good, for salvation, for doing God's will. Anything less is a perversion, perhaps even a sin.

Beauty in the service of justice: that's an exciting concept, and a healing one. God calls us to use whatever beauty we have to bring justice to his people. He asks that we look for issues larger than our own mirrors and then to act on what we see.

Susannah and Bathsheba

The stories of Susannah and Bathsheba are quite different, yet much in them is the same. That they are brought together here is a caution. Your beauty can be used against you, no matter how virtuous you may be. Both these women endured much because of their beauty. The healing message is that both these women endured.

Susannah, you may recall, was accused of being sexually immoral, though nothing could have been more false.

She was saved by the judicial brilliance of Daniel of lions' den fame when it appeared that she would have to die for her "crime." But it is saddening to read the words the author has put into Daniel's mouth. Even as he declared and celebrated her innocence, the prejudices of history color his words in a sad way. As he castigated the men who had conspired against her because she would not comply with their sexual demands on her, he said, "beauty has beguiled you and lust has perverted your heart" (Dan 13:56-57).

How truly awful that lust and beauty are held equally to blame. How wrong! How unfair! Lust is a deliberate violation of the ninth commandment. It is a sin, a choice for evil. It has nothing to do with accident or goodness. Scripture even tells us that the men who lusted after Susannah "suppressed their consciences" and "turned away their eyes from looking to heaven or remembering their duty to administer justice" (Dan 13:9). They preferred their lust to righteousness.

On the other hand, there is beauty, a gift from God to Susannah who was a woman who "feared the Lord"; she was trained "according to the law of Moses" (Dan 13:2-3). The story reveals her modesty, her reverence for her own beauty as—preparing to bathe—she told her maids to "shut the garden doors" (Dan 13:17) to give her privacy. Susannah was simply beautiful, yet that beauty came to be equated with lust. Lust subverted. Beauty seduced.

Now the writer of Daniel surely did not seriously intend to criticize Susannah. But the language used illustrates the basic flaw in our subconscious thinking. To be beautiful is to be guilty. To be beautiful is to incite sexual aggression. To be beautiful is to cause sin. We might as well say that it's the trout's fault that it gets eaten because it tastes so good.

Refuse the guilt. Reject the thinking. Beauty is not a fault, not a temptation, not a crime. It is a great gift. Enjoy it, and put it at the service of God.

Then we have Bathsheba. It's interesting to note that in both stories the women are being spied upon while they are bathing. Somehow, and it may have to do with the movies, despite what Scripture has to say, the image of Bathsheba as seductress has come about. But in fact, nothing could be less true about Bathsheba, wife of Uriah, and a woman who was "very beautiful" (2 Sam 11:2). David saw her and desired her despite having been told that she was someone else's wife; he desired her so much that he sent messengers who "took her" to the palace (2 Sam 11:4) where he had sexual relations with her. The text doesn't suggest that she sought such a liaison, much less that she plotted to bring it about. Yet the image has arisen and continues to dominate much of our thinking about her.

But let's pursue the story of this woman whose beauty proved to be someone else's excuse for piling sin upon sin. When David had finished with her, he allowed her to return home and the story might have ended there. But Bathsheba found herself pregnant and, in dismay as countless women before and after her have done, she told the father of the child.

Bathsheba's husband had been away for many months and could not possibly have been the father. So David conspired to have him killed. We are told, "When the wife of Uriah heard that her husband was dead, she made lamentation for him" (2 Sam 11:26). It is apparent once more that this was a virtuous woman who had been forced to do something against the wishes of her heart. Further, "once the mourning was over, David sent and brought her to his house" (2 Sam 11:27). There is no word that Bathsheba, now pregnant and a widow, pursued him. But popular history has branded her a seductress.

She was a woman, a beautiful woman. Therefore, it was her fault, just like Eve, just like Susannah, and just like the attitude we too often find toward rape victims and battered wives. Beauty has been interpreted as an invitation to violence.

Could this have been what God intended? It seems ridiculous even to ask that question.

Toward Healing

As Vashti and Esther illustrate, at least part of the reason God created beauty was for the doing of truth and justice. As Susannah and Bathsheba illustrate, God's vision can be perverted. But if we look to the two Persian queens and listen to their words, watch their actions, and pray for light, we will find healing for our own wounded beauty. If we pay close attention to Susannah and Bathsheba we can refuse guilt that is not rightly ours when others trespass against us.

Prayer

Creator God of all that is beautiful, I thank you for my own gift of beauty. I embrace the beauty of my womanhood and I desire to learn from you how it may serve your will.

Help me to remember that beauty is given for salvation, for the doing of justice and goodness, for upholding my dignity as a woman. When others would make me an object, O God, I pray for the grace to reject that vision, and I pray that that vision may be changed. Let me always walk in your vision for me: a woman gifted for the fulfillment of your desire for all the earth.

If others have done violence to me against my will because of my beauty, my womanhood, I ask for the grace to forgive them and to find a way of turning that experience into a positive good. Only you can help me to do that, God, and I know that you will. So I thank you.

Vashti, Esther, Susannah and Bathsheba, pray for me and for the beauty of all creation. Amen.

Chapter Three

Ruth and Naomi

The Power and Promise of Friendship

The story of Ruth and Naomi is one of the most healing stories of the Old Testament. This story is as familiar to me as my own name. When I first began to read the Bible, I started with Ruth, for obvious reasons. What a blessed choice it was. For in this story we discover not only what a gift it is to be a woman, but what gifts other women are to us as well.

We start with what almost seems to be a dead end: Ruth and Naomi, mother-in-law and daughter-in-law. All the jokes about that kind of doomed relationship come to mind. If we pursue the story, however, we find that these two are often the absolute antithesis of the jokes, the complete opposite of what we have been taught, explicitly or otherwise, about what is likely or even possible between and among women.

What I'd like to do is to go through the story with you in less Biblical terms, to try to make it more real to us, less like something that could only happen in ancient times to people who were beyond anything we can understand. Put in the words of our time and culture, the story reveals that Ruth and Naomi are not women locked in history, but women for today who present a wonderful challenge to us in our time.

How It Began

The story of Ruth began with a famine in the land of Judah. The famine was so severe that Naomi, her husband and their two sons traveled to the land of Moab to search for a place where they could live. They settled there. Both sons married Moabite women, one named Orpha and the other named Ruth. The story is told so simply in the Bible that perhaps we don't take time to realize just what all that meant to them.

The people of Israel looked down on the Moabites as foreigners. It would seem likely that when this family from Bethlehem moved to Moab, the sons would have made certain to take Israelite wives with them. Instead, they chose to marry Moabites—foreigners and aliens. That says a lot about Naomi's family. They were willing to venture out of their own tradition.

That they did not marry Moabite men says a great deal about Ruth and Orpha. They were willing to take a chance on entering a family and a culture that were very strange to them. These two young women had great courage. They were open to the will of God who was willing to work wonders even among the "unchosen" of his people.

The Return to Bethlehem

Naomi's husband soon died, and about ten years later both her sons died as well. This left Naomi lost and alone in this country of Moab with her two Moabite daughters-in-law. Then Naomi heard that the famine had ended in Judah, so she decided to return to her homeland. We don't know how long she stayed in Moab, but we do know it had been a long time. How could she be certain of the reception she would find in Bethlehem? How would things have changed? What kinfolk might or might not still be alive? But in faith she set out, accompanied by Ruth and Orpha.

On their way to Bethlehem, Naomi began to realize that her daughters-in-law might find a very cool welcome. Remember, Moabites were regarded as "less than" by the people of Israel. So Naomi stopped and said to them:

"I appreciate what you are doing by coming with me, but it's really not necessary. When I get to Bethlehem, I'll be back among my husband's kin and my own family. I'll be all right. But it will be hard for you. Why don't you two return to your parents, to your own people, to a lifestyle and culture you understand? Go back and be happy. Coming with me holds no promise for you. I don't have any more sons, and even if I gave birth to a son now, you would be old ladies by the time he was grown. Do yourselves a favor and go back."

Orpha must have paused to consider her choice. Her heart was good. She evidently loved Naomi, or she wouldn't have started out on the journey with her. But the advice the older woman gave seemed wise, logical and practical. So she turned back to Moab and went home.

But Ruth? Ruth was not so practical. More intuitive and perhaps more compassionate than her sister-in-law, Ruth continued on to Bethlehem. Orpha returned to Moab and disappeared from history. Ruth, the visionary, listened to her heart, went on, and earned a permanent place in the story of our salvation.

I doubt that she did it without some qualms. She must have looked back and thought how good it would be to go home, back where everybody understood her and she understood them. She looked ahead and saw that she was heading to a strange land, where she had no idea what she would find. Besides her lower class status as a woman, she would be taking on the yoke of being a foreigner and thus a minority. She must have trembled inwardly as she considered her prospects.

A Contemporary Example

My own sister had a similar experience. She married an African, and they lived in New York for the first few years of their marriage. Even though she had married outside her race and culture, she had the comfort of living in her own country, with her own language and customs, where she was at home in the fullest sense of that word.

But then her husband was sent back to Africa, and naturally he expected her to come with him. She looked ahead and saw that she would be going to a country that was quite poor, and which had been torn by civil war for many years. People there generally did not speak English, and she did not know their language. This nation had an entirely different set of customs in which her husband would be very much at home, but where she would be a stranger.

Despite it all, she went with him, just as Ruth went with Naomi. Having listened to my sister's doubts and hesitations before she left for Africa, I can't help but feel that Ruth also had a lot of questions about what Bethlehem would be like. What would she find there? Would happiness even be possible? But real love is greater than doubt. So my sister went...and so did Ruth.

Whither Thou Goest

Ruth's moving words form one of the most famous passages in the Bible: "Do not press me to leave you or to turn back from following you! Where you go, I will go; where you lodge, I will lodge; your people shall be my people, and your God my God. Where you die, I will die— there will I be buried" (Ruth 1:16-17).

This speech has been used as a love song for weddings. But it's important to remember that this was not a man speaking to a woman or a woman speaking to a man. This was a woman speaking to another woman, a daughter-in-law speaking to her mother-in-law, making a commitment in a total pledge of love.

In effect Ruth said, "Wherever you live is fine by me. I'll live there too. I will take your people, your friends and your relatives for my own. Your God, the God of Israel, the God of Abraham and Sarah, of Isaac and Rebecca, will be my God too."

Those are powerful words for anyone, but quite remarkable for one woman to say to another. Would it happen now? Perhaps it might on occasion, but more probably it wouldn't. We've been raised with endless mother-in-law stories, so that when we marry we usually don't expect to be best friends with our mothers-in-law. Of course there are exceptions, and some in-law relationships thrive, but they seem to be in the minority. In such a relationship we often expect tension, dislike and mistrust.

It's unusual to find such absolute devotion between any two women. Ruth's words were a pledge, an act of trust that appears rash from our perspective. Our upbringing may have taught us that other women won't ever be our real friends, because we are competing with each other for a man.

Happily, a generation is now growing up in which this kind of thinking is not nearly so pervasive. But those of us who were affected by it must be honest enough to admit how we feel if we are to be healed. It's difficult to be that honest with ourselves, but it's also necessary for healing to begin. When I confronted this in myself, I was startled and ashamed. But it was our God, working through Ruth, who helped me get in touch with it and healed me of that unkind and limiting expectation.

Expectations

The great power in this story is that it explodes some myths about women, about how they relate with each other, and about the expectations that have developed from such myths as: women cannot really be friends; women cannot really trust one another; mothers-in-law and daughters-in-law are doomed to dislike.

Could such outlooks become self-fulfilling prophecies? We believe the myths and we form the expectations, and then what we expect comes to pass. Women do not trust; women do not love one another; women in-laws live in a state of armed tension. Our expectations are realized.

History has provided us with the expectations, the boxes and the tombs. It has defined who we are and are not and how we will and will not relate to one another. We have wrapped those definitions around ourselves like a winding sheet, have jumped into the box and helped to nail it shut.

Far from being freeing and life-giving, expectations are tombs in which we encase ourselves, others and God. Then we throw away the keys and wonder why things are as they are.

Possibilities

Naomi and Ruth put the lie to that posture, those expectations of enemy, of competitor. They show that we can forge greater loyalties and greater trusts. They prove that real bonding and friendship can exist among women, a friendship that transcends the competition and empties the in-law jokes of their meaning. As the story of Ruth and Naomi develops, we discover that their friendship led, however indirectly, to the greatest gift this world has ever received: Jesus Christ.

That gift came from the bonding of those two women. It was a bonding that never would have occurred had Ruth and Naomi allowed themselves to become victims of expectations. They might have stifled some of their greatest possibilities and, like Orpha, would have disappeared into oblivion. But they didn't. They were open to the Spirit and so to their mutual potential in relationship.

That relationship made Ruth's trip to Bethlehem possible. It made Ruth and Boaz possible. Therefore, it made King David possible, and ultimately made Jesus possible. It's not that God couldn't have found another way. But Ruth and Naomi furthered the divine plan, because they were not entombed in expectations but were free to act in accordance with the will of God.

Living in a graveyard of expectations forces us to cram everything that happens and everyone we experience into that graveyard. Anything or anyone who refuses to fit must be eliminated. This is the thinking that sent Jesus to the cross. He simply didn't fit into the mold of what was expected of a Messiah. This is the thinking that keeps us living in and among the tombs.

Why do we do it? Because it's safer, of course. We don't have to worry about the possibility of being challenged to grow in ways that might be uncomfortable. We have set our limits in advance. We set limits on others. This may give us the illusion of control but it lets no miracles happen.

The Truth Will Set You Free

When Jesus was on earth, he said, "You will know the truth, and the truth will make you free" (Jn 8:32). I think he was talking about much more than we might realize. Yes, he set us free from sin. He set us free from the power of evil. He set us free from so many things. Not least of the freedoms he offers is freedom from the tomb of expectations, that tomb which is not of the truth, that terrible tomb which keeps us from discovering the awesome joy of freedom.

Jesus is standing outside all our tombs right now and calling us to come out into freedom. Can we resist? Can women be friends? They can and they must. When they do, incredible and wonderful things take place. Miracles can happen, just as they did for Ruth and Naomi.

Meanwhile in Bethlehem

What follows in the story indicates that Ruth and Naomi were fairly poor on their return to Bethlehem. Ruth offers to go out and glean behind the reapers. This was something the poor did because it was a privilege guaranteed to them by the Mosaic law (cf. Lev 19:9-10). They followed behind those who were gathering the harvest and collected whatever was overlooked or left behind. In this way they were able to make bread and to get enough to eat.

With Naomi's consent, Ruth went out to glean. God laid a mighty hand on future developments because the field in which Ruth chose to work just "by chance" belonged to Boaz, a kinsman of Naomi.

As things develop, Boaz notices Ruth among the gleaners. Just as Ruth proves to be an exceptional human being, so does Boaz. He is moved by her dedication to her work and probably to some extent by her beauty, and he tells her to stay in his fields until the harvest is finished, gleaning behind his reapers. Further, he assures her that, at his order, no harm will come to her from the young men. He instructs his servants to leave plenty behind in their gathering to make certain that Ruth finds enough to feed herself and Naomi.

What motivated him to do this? "All that you have done for your mother-in-law since the death of your husband has been fully told me," he says (Ruth 2:11). Such womanly loyalty must have been uncommon enough even then to arouse admiration when it occurred.

The Law of Next-of-Kin

When Naomi discovers that Boaz has taken an interest in Ruth, she coaches Ruth in the law. She tells her particularly about the law as it regards marrying a widow's next-of-kin (Deut 25:5). She tells Ruth to lie at Boaz' feet that night after he has retired. Ruth does so and, when Boaz discovers her, points out to him that he is her close kinsman through Naomi. Boaz responds to her openness and loyalty to him and, overcoming certain obstacles which are not important here, he marries her. Their child Obed in time became the father of Jesse, and Jesse became the father of King David.

The point here is that Naomi and Ruth continued to

support one another and to care for one another in every way possible. Still young and attractive, Ruth probably could have found a husband from among the young men of Bethlehem. Naomi might even have been able to claim Boaz herself, as he was not a young man and he was her kinsman. But the women had become such fast friends that they put their own friendship above all other considerations.

Theirs was a bond of mutual love and protection. Ruth sought to protect Naomi from the solitude of a lonely old age and from the dangers of hunger. Naomi sought to protect Ruth's virtue and future. They were courageous women. Naomi was brave enough to return to Bethlehem with a "foreign" daughter-in-law; Ruth was brave enough to challenge Boaz gently to do his duty as her kinsman.

In their great friendship they shared the bitter draught of death and poverty. In their great friendship they found a reward of sweetness and mutual triumph. Naomi had a grandchild to cherish, and Ruth and Boaz gave birth to a dynasty that culminated in the Savior of the world. Such is the power of women *with* women.

Prayer

Loving God, I thank you for the story of Ruth and Naomi. I thank you for the grace to realize that all women, young and old, are my potential friends. I thank you that they teach me the depths of love which women can have for one another, and I thank you that they show me what is possible as I discover the truth of my own womanhood.

I ask you now for the blessing of friendship, for the blessing of an open heart, for the blessing of trust in those women who companion me now and who will companion me in the future. Help me to remember all that we are and all that we can be when we allow ourselves to love.

Most gracious Giver of Gifts, help me also to remember those women who still must glean behind the harvesters. I ask the grace to be ever conscious that they are my sisters too. Lead those of us women who have plenty, to show concern for those who have little.

Ruth and Naomi, pray for me and for all your sisters on earth. Amen.

Chapter Four

The Women Who Laughed

Rejoicing in the Unexpectedness of God

A time comes in every woman's life, indeed, in the life of every human being, when we feel settled. "This is it. This is how my life is—and will be. This is how things are." Sometimes we feel good about that and sometimes we don't. Either way is not the holiest way to live. If we want to be women in all the fullness of that word, then we cannot close ourselves off. We must remain open to the Spirit, to the holiness of surprise. God has a way of unexpectedly popping in and out and changing things and people in most amazing ways. Take, for example, the women who laughed!

The very idea of God using a woman to change or influence salvation history can cause laughter. We know that we are very rarely powerful people. Yet heaven and earth are filled with the laughter of all the women God has caught and is catching in the holy net of surprise ...sometimes the best and brightest women...and more often the very least.

The Barren

"Now Abraham and Sarah were old, advanced in age; it had ceased to be with Sarah after the manner of women" (Gen 18:11). This must have caused some doubt and distress. Hadn't God promised Abraham that he would father a host of nations (cf. Gen 17:5) and that his descendants would be as numerous as the stars (cf. Gen 15:5)?

Yet the years went by and no children were born to them, only Ishmael, son of Abraham and Hagar, Sarah's Egyptian maidservant. Then one day, three men came to Abraham and told him that by the next year Sarah and Abraham would have a son.

Scripture then tells us that Sarah laughed to herself at the idea (cf. Gen 18:12), just as Abraham had laughed earlier when God promised the one hundred-year-old patriarch and his ninety-year-old wife a child (cf. Gen 17:17). Laughter accompanied the announcement of the pregnancy and laughter decided the name of the child, Isaac (cf. Gen 21:3), which means "to laugh." "Now Sarah said, 'God has brought laughter for me; everyone who hears will laugh with me'" (Gen 21:6).

Unlike Sarah, Hannah never gave up hope. She had been married to Elkanah for many years and, though Elkanah's other wife had children, Hannah remained barren (cf. 1 Sam 1:5). Hannah always reminds me of the woman in Jesus' parable who wanted justice and continued to hound the judge until she got it (cf. Lk 18:1-8). Hannah wanted a child and refused to give up hope of having one.

The story tells us that Hannah prayed long and hard and with such desperation that Eli, a priest in the temple, thought she was drunk (cf. 1 Sam 1:13-14). But Hannah explained her desperation and received Eli's blessing. She also obviously received the blessing of God, for she soon conceived and gave birth to Samuel.

Scripture doesn't say explicitly that she laughed. But how could she not? Her faith had sustained her. Her God had heard her. Her womb had unexpectedly filled with a child. Hannah laughed!

Rachel was another woman who stood by in sadness as her husband's other wife Leah bore child after child. Rachel remained barren (cf. Gen 29:31) and what pain it must have caused her. It was only after many years, during which Leah bore six sons and a daughter, that Rachel at last conceived and bore a son whom she named Joseph.

She cried out, "God has taken away my reproach" (Gen 30:23). I believe that Rachel also laughed.

Rebekah, wife of Isaac and daughter-in-law of Abraham, was still another woman who seemed to have little cause for joy. For twenty years after their marriage, she and Isaac waited for a child. Isaac prayed that she be delivered from her barrenness (cf. Gen 25:21). Finally she did conceive and gave birth, not to one son but to the twins, Esau and Jacob. Who would not laugh at such great fortune?

We do not know her name, but the wife of Manoah also "was barren, having borne no children" (Jgs 13:2). Again God broke in with a surprise. An angel appeared to her and said, "Although you are barren, having borne no children, you shall conceive and bear a son" (Jgs 13:3). So she did. In the fullness of her time she gave birth to Samson, and we can still hear her laughter of delight ringing through the ages.

The Unlikely

During the reign of Antiochus Epiphanes, the king unleashed a fearful persecution against the Jews. He profaned their holy places, abolished their law, forbade circumcision, prevented the keeping of the sabbath, and demanded that they eat "unclean" foods. He punished with a terrible death anyone who transgressed any of his rules (cf. 2 Macc 1-9).

"It happened also that seven brothers and their mother were arrested and were being compelled by the king, under torture with whips and thongs, to partake of unlawful swine's flesh" (2 Macc 7:1). One by one the brothers refused and were tortured to death before the eyes of their mother. Each brother in turn spoke out bravely against Antiochus and for the God of their belief.

> The mother was especially admirable and worthy of honorable memory. Although she saw her seven sons perish within a single day, she bore it with good courage because of her hope in the Lord. She encouraged each of them in the language of their ancestors. Filled with a noble spirit, she reinforced her woman's reasoning with a man's courage, and said to them, "I do not know how you came into being in my womb. It was not I who gave you life and breath, nor I who set in order the elements within each of you. Therefore the Creator of the world, who shaped the beginning of humankind and devised the origin of all things, will in his mercy give life and breath back to you again, since you now forget yourselves for the sake of his laws" (2 Macc 7:20-23).

Finally, after watching each of her sons die and exhorting them not to be afraid but to go bravely to God, she too was martyred (cf. 2 Macc 7:41).

What a woman! What an unlikely woman! She was a woman alone, probably a widow since the text says that she had brought up her seventh son, educated and supported him (cf. 2 Macc 7:27). As a woman and mother, probably she would not have been as much criticized as a man had she caved in to the demands of the king. But she knew her role as a woman and as a mother: to be nurturer, teacher and *exemplar*. When God broke into her "womanly" heart, he found fertile ground and gave her the courage of the Holy Spirit, empowering her to laugh in the face of danger. So this unnamed and unlikely woman became a sign for all of Israel of their covenant with God, their surprising God, their God whose Spirit blows where it will. Dare we call that Spirit capricious?

The "Cursed"

Then there was Sarah, daughter of Raguel and Edna. Sarah was hounded by the demon Asmodeus who had killed all seven of the men she had married before any of the marriages could be consummated (cf. Tob 3:8). Sarah was considered cursed by God and even thought of taking her own life. What held her back was her great love for her parents, on whom she would not lay that ignominious sorrow. So she prayed that God would let her die or, if not, that he would look favorably and have pity on her (cf. Tob 3:11-15).

God heard her prayer and caused Tobiah to be led to her. He loved her immediately and married her, knowing her history but believing also that he was doing the will of God. Asmodeus was repelled and the young lovers prayed in thanksgiving and hope. Their marriage was consummated safely and they truly lived "happily ever after."

Sarah had lost seven husbands but lived to give birth to seven sons (cf. Tob 14:3). Her faith in her God had removed the curse, and her laughter echoed throughout the city of Media.

The Weak

Our surprising God broke in again through the voice of a servant girl. The story begins....

> Naaman, commander of the army of the king of Aram, was a great man and in high favor with his master, because by him the Lord had given victory to Aram. The man, though a mighty warrior, suffered from leprosy. Now the Arameans on one of their raids had taken a young girl captive from the land of Israel, and she served Naaman's wife. She said to her mistress, "If only my lord were with the prophet who is in Samaria! He would cure him of his leprosy." So Naaman went in and told his lord just what the girl from the land of Israel had said (2 Kgs 5:1-4).

Humanity being prey to all sorts of pride, many "ins and outs" follow. But in the end Naaman was cured and, even more important, was converted to the God of Israel. "Now I know that there is no God in all the earth, except in Israel" (2 Kgs 5:15).

Though we are not told so directly, the servant girl must have been rewarded. How could she help but laugh?

The Foreigner

Joseph of the coat-of-many-colors is a man whose story we all know. But how many of us remember that this most remarkable man was married to a "foreigner," an Egyptian woman named Asenath, the daughter of Potiphera, priest of Heliopolis (cf. Gen 41:45)? Through her he had two sons, Manasseh and Ephraim (cf. Gen 41:50-52). We know nothing else about her, but her name lives, a vibrant part of Israel's history as the mother of two of the twelve tribes.

There were other women who doubtless laughed as God broke in unexpectedly and changed their lives forever. Scripture is a garden rich with these stories. God invites you to discover them for yourselves.

God Breaks into Our Stories

Why are these stories so frequent in Scripture? What meaning do they hold for us today?

Remember at the beginning of this chapter the mention of the "unexpectedness" of God? Remember, too, the reference to our too common resignation to things as they are? What does all this have to do with our being women, women in need of healing?

I believe it has a great deal to do with our womanhood, our ability to give life, and our perceived weakness, powerlessness and "foreignness" to what is considered a more desirable way of being. It has to do with God who doesn't see us in negative ways at all, but sees our potential for participating in his plan for all humankind's salvation. It has to do with God's delighting in the unexpected.

God breaks into our stories again and again no matter how lifeless they might seem, how barren, how doomed, how humble and powerless, in order that his will might be accomplished. But I also think that he does it to bring us delight and the gift of laughter.

If we have even an inkling of God, we know that "this" doesn't ever have to be "it." We know that being woman is to be a gift to creation. We shouldn't think that we are too sterile, too old, too set in our ways, too foreign, too weak, too unlikely for exciting and joyful things to happen to us.

But there is a proviso. We must be as open as were all these women to accepting the seed God wishes to plant within us, that seed that is usually unexpected and always gives new life, new possibilities, and even makes us new.

God is always calling us to join with him in birthing and mothering newness and in healing what has been wounded in ourselves and others. When we are young, it's easy to follow the call. We are still spontaneous and energetic and eager for life. But as the years grind by, we begin to slow down. We are more careful. Birthing of any kind seems to be a tremendous effort, perhaps more effort than we care to make. We become sterile. Mothering seems to call for hardiness and courage, perhaps too much hardiness, too demanding a courage. Healing can come to be too difficult and taxing. Perhaps things are better left as they are. Then we become as barren as the fig tree (cf. Lk 13:6-9). We no longer yield any kind of fruit.

That is the real danger of limiting our horizons and dwelling in tombs of negative expectations: giving up hope and quenching our dreams, settling for what is, rather than striving for what might be. For God's sake and our own, we must not let that happen. We must remain as open as wives to their husbands to the exciting and surprising seed of God.

It's the flash that says, "Is this all there is?" It's the spark that cries, "This is *not* it!" It's the moment of wondering, "What if?" At those times, our God of the unexpected is breaking through, urging us to accept the seed of the divinely possible.

Granted, it may take a lot of time and energy, just as pregnancy usually does. It may cause some discomfort and even pain, just as giving birth does. It will probably take patience, as healing always does. But it brings new life where there was barrenness. That is something at which we women excel.

New life—the promise of God that "The wilderness and the dry land shall be glad, the desert shall rejoice and blossom; like the crocus it shall blossom abundantly, and rejoice with joy and singing" (Is 35:1-2). It is the sudden and surprising fulfillment of the promise. Then we will laugh and laugh and laugh again.

Prayer

God of laughter and surprises, I thank you now for all the laughter I have enjoyed in my life and for all the times you have surprised me into newness. I want to thank you for the birthing times and the sudden realizations of your presence, not at some great and impossible distance, but here in my heart, in my life.

I want to thank you, too, for the moments of courage I have had and for the things you have enabled me to accomplish, even when I wasn't certain I had the power to accomplish anything at all. I thank you for the healing of my fear and uncertainty even now as I speak with you.

I ask for the grace to stay open to you and the seeds of life that you plant within me. I ask for the grace to keep on believing in my own possibilities in you, even when it seems that circumstances or age are against me. Help me to keep faith in your promise and your constant love for me.

Please, God of laughter, help me to loose my own joy, to let it spread like honey across my life and into others' lives, that they will know the sweetness and delight that you are. Let me be love and laughter for as much of the world as I can touch.

All you women of surprised laughter, please pray for me and for all women. Amen.

Chapter Five

The Heroine in Ourselves
The Vocation of Woman

Heroine! What a wonderful word that is, conjuring up images of a strong and powerful woman capable of accomplishing amazing things. Wouldn't it be fantastic to be a heroine? For a moment our imaginations drift.

Then we sigh and look at beds to be made, dishes to be washed, budgets to be balanced, correspondence to be answered, kids to be carpooled, and business appointments to be juggled. The world of the powerful heroine seems far away indeed.

But stop for a moment. Are you sure you can't be a heroine? Are you really powerless? Or has your true power been put into some sort of historical costume that renders it impotent, equating women with weakness. For one long minute, look at what history has told us.

It was usually the men who wielded great power. Women did as they were told. If a woman did somehow manage to take power, more often than not she embraced the "masculine" to such an extent that she became the worst of that, not the best. For example, Catherine the Great murdered with impunity, and Elizabeth I referred to herself as "king." Those are not exactly inviting heroines for those of us who prefer the more feminine virtues.

Even the stories we were told as children reinforced our stereotypes of weak and helpless women. From Sleeping Beauty to Rapunzel to Cinderella, all waited, willingly or not, to be rescued, saved and carried off in the arms of the hero.

Is it any wonder, then, that we cannot see ourselves as powerful heroines, and that we too often sit back and wait for someone else to bring about a better world?

The time for sitting and waiting is past, if it ever existed. We must take charge of our own destinies and our ability to influence both the present and the future. We are neither helpless nor captive...unless we choose to be. We have power, our own particular kind of power, power to do good, power that comes when we are faithful to our womanhood and all that means in terms of our passion for life.

Scripture gives us many examples of powerful women who were filled with woman-power, a gift quite different from its masculine counterpart. Some of those women are familiar: Esther, Ruth, Susannah. But others are the unsung whose names are not well-known, but whose effect on the human drama has been great. They are heroines of our past and exemplars for our present. They reveal to us not just who *they* were, but who *we* are. They give life to our possibilities.

Rahab: The Courageous

For instance, turn to the book of Joshua. If you're as typical as I, your knowledge of Joshua probably begins and ends with the idea that somehow the walls of Jericho came tumbling down under the assault of Joshua and his armies. While not taking anything away from his victory, I would like to suggest that the "somehow" was really the power of God, working through a "someone" named Rahab.

Rahab was a prostitute in Jericho. When Joshua sent spies to reconnoiter the situation in that city, they chose to stay with Rahab. Rahab had heard of the God of Israel, and she believed him to be a mighty God. So when the king of Jericho demanded that she turn Joshua's spies over to him, she hid them instead and lied to the king, telling him that they had already left Jericho.

That night Rahab crept up to the roof of her house where she had hidden the spies "with the stalks of flax that she had laid out on the roof" (Jos 2:6). She made a bargain with them. She would get them safely out of the city if, when they attacked and conquered it, they would protect her and her family. The spies agreed. (Read Joshua 2 through 6 for all the intricacies of the bargain and the attack.)

Attentive to Yahweh even in her sinfulness, Rahab showed tremendous courage and tremendous womanhood. She risked her life, not for power or riches or glory, but only for the safety of her family. This seems to be a most womanly response, a life-giving response, and one that affected the history of Israel in more ways than one.

Rahab's bargain facilitated the occupation of Canaan, certainly an important moment for God's chosen people. "But Rahab the prostitute, with her family and all who belonged to her, Joshua spared. Her family has lived in Israel ever since. For she hid the messengers whom Joshua sent to spy out Jericho" (cf. Jos 6:25).

If you now turn to Matthew 1:5, you will find that Rahab the prostitute became the mother of Boaz, husband of Ruth, and so the great-great-grandmother of King David, of whose house Jesus was born. She preserved her life, her family and her name without sacrificing her womanliness for one moment.

Rahab's story holds healing for us, for she reminds us that the ways of greatness are not always what the world would have us think. Too often we equate greatness with prestige and political or financial power. But Rahab illustrates that true greatness can consist in something as simple as choosing life for her family. She points out for all of us that immense riches or occupational prestige are illusory power, as the king of Jericho soon came to realize. True power is in giving and protecting life. It is a power that is natural to women, and this power can affect the course of history.

If every woman were to call on that power today, what changes might be wrought...from the White House to the humblest dwellings in the poorest nations! So as we remember Esther, let us also remember Rahab and make our choice, our powerful choice for life.

Shiphrah and Puah: The Resistant

Now turn to Exodus 1:15, and take pride in your heritage as woman. Shiphrah and Puah were Hebrew midwives in Egypt when the Israelites were enslaved there. They played only a small part in a much bigger story about Pharaoh and his daughter and Moses, but they shine like twin stars in God's plan for saving his people.

Right at the beginning of Exodus we find them being told quite specifically by Pharaoh to murder any baby boy born to a Hebrew woman, because Pharaoh was concerned about the great number of male children being born into slavery. "But the midwives feared God; they did not do as the king of Egypt commanded them, but they let the boys live" (Ex 1:17).

'Was this the beginning of "passive resistance"? Women acted as women. They preserved life, refused death, and put their own lives at risk for a greater good. That is the courage and strength of the "weaker sex." That is the courage and strength God has given us for life.

It takes courage and strength to resist our cultural values: to turn off offensive television programs and to let the sponsors know; to teach the virtue of purity to sexually-blooming young people; to choose a career for its ministerial possibilities instead of its financial rewards; to be the kind of parent or child or friend we know in our hearts God would want us to be. But we have that strength and that courage. We have only to remember Shiphrah and Puah to be certain of that.

The Levite Mother, the Watchful Sister, and Pharaoh's Daughter: Deliverers of Israel

The story recounted in Exodus 2:1-10 is short and familiar. It tells how Pharaoh's daughter found a Hebrew baby hidden in the Nile, rescued him, and raised him to be a prince of Egypt. But how often have we given much more than a moment's thought to those three women— the mother, the sister, the princess—as genuine heroines?

It is no small thing to defy a Pharaoh, especially when defiance can mean death. But just as Shiphrah and Puah, that is exactly what Jochebed, the mother of Moses did (cf. Ex 6:20). God had written on her heart already what her son would speak in Yahweh's name so many years later. "Choose life so that you and your descendants may live" (Deut 30:19). So Jochebed chose life. She chose the warm and breathing body of her son over the rigid and sharp-edged letters of Pharaoh's words. She did it in a woman's way, allowing her imagination to unfold a path of "creative obedience."

We read that "Pharaoh commanded all his people, 'Every boy that is born to the Hebrews you shall throw into the Nile, but you shall let every girl live'" (Ex 1:22). So the mother made a basket, put the baby inside it, and put it among the reeds in the river. Was this the letter of the law? It was in a way, but it was a letter made round and soft by the coming of the Spirit. The Levite mother was a woman in touch with her holy call to be life-bearing and life-giving and she claimed her power to be so.

In the telescopic language of Scripture, what is one of the most dramatic scenes in the Old Testament is then told in a matter of four verses.

> His sister stood at a distance, to see what would happen to him. The daughter of Pharaoh came down to bathe at the river, while her attendants walked beside the river. She saw the basket among the reeds and sent her maid to bring it. When she opened it, she saw the child. He was crying, and she took pity on him. "This must be one of the Hebrews' children," she said. Then his sister said to Pharaoh's daughter, "Shall I go and get you a nurse from the Hebrew women to nurse the child for you?" (Ex 2:4-7)

Those are the bare bones of the story. Let us give them flesh.

That the sister Miriam (cf. Ex 6:20) loved her little brother passionately is without question. Why else would she place herself in such danger, close enough to guard him and, so, close enough to be discovered herself? Her mother seems to have relinquished him to the care of God. But not the sister. She waited and watched and wondered. What thoughts might have crossed her mind? What hopes or plans might have nestled in her heart? We can only guess, but whatever those thoughts and hopes and plans were, we can be certain that she was determined to keep the child safe.

Then came—not, as Miriam feared, a crocodile—but the princess! What was the sister to do? Again she waited. Perhaps the princess would not notice. Too late! The basket was discovered and a curious princess opened it. What did it contain? A baby! A baby boy! Instantly the princess understood. It was a Hebrew child whose life was more precious to its mother than the mother's own. It was a Hebrew boy. By royal edict it must die. But how can this princess, this woman, looking into the tiny face, cast the child into the river? What is she to do, obey her father...or defy him?

Then the sister appeared. No words are recorded, no pleas for the innocent life. Probably there were none. The richly clad and privileged princess and the dirty and disheveled slave faced one another across the child in the basket. All their life-giving womanhood was in that look and the baby was saved. There was no need for conversation. The heroine in each was revealed and a man of great destiny was allowed to live.

That settled, the sister, wise beyond her years, spoke, offering to find a nurse. The princess, also wise, agreed, and the baby was returned to his mother.

What irony this story holds. The mighty Pharaoh sought to destroy the strength of Israel by having its men killed at birth. That thinking proved ultimately to be his undoing. As this story and others tell us, the strength of Israel in chains was often in its women!

I have found such healing in this story: healing of my doubts when faith is needed; healing of my fears of people and things seemingly more powerful than I; healing of my reluctance to put myself in the path of "danger" when safety means abandoning someone who is weaker than I.

As Jochebed left her child in the basket and in the care of God, so we must learn sometimes, having done our best, to let go of control and have faith that God will take care of the situation. As Miriam put aside her own fears of accusation and punishment in order to keep watch over the infant boy, so must we be willing to endure the risk of exposure and ridicule, in order to keep guard over what we know is truth. Just as Pharaoh's daughter was willing to unleash the wrath of her father in order to protect the life of a child, so must we be willing to unleash the wrath of the abortion-makers to protect the lives of those not yet able to help themselves.

As we allow the mother, the sister, the princess to touch our lives in our times of prayer and contemplation, we are made stronger in our womanhood and more ready to become the necessary heroines of our time and place.

The Daughters of Zelophehad:
Seekers of Justice

Then the daughters of Zelophehad came forward. Zelophehad was son of Hepher, son of Gilead, son of Machir, son of Manasseh, son of Joseph, a member of the Manassite clans. The names of his daughters were: Mahlah, Noah, Hoglah, Milcah and Tirzah. They stood before Moses, Eleazar the priest, the leaders, and all the congregation, at the entrance of the tent of meeting, and they said, "Our father died in the wilderness; he was not among the company of those who gathered themselves together against the Lord in the company of Korah, but died for his own sin; and he had no sons. Why should the name of our father be taken away from his clan because he had no son? Give to us a possession among our father's brothers" (Num 27:1-4).

In effect, these women were about to be declared "non-persons." Even their family name was to be eradicated. They pleaded for justice, and they dared to challenge the law and the custom of their society in order to have it. On the surface it would appear that they had no power. They were merely women in a society that did not grant them any sort of equality. But in the name of justice, they dared to band together and to speak out. They had power because they banded together.

One woman alone may not have the strength to fight the system, or a voice loud enough to be heard. But a group possesses power, a power that is stronger than the sum of the individual parts. The daughters of Zelophehad knew this and took advantage of it in their quest for justice.

What boldness! What audacity! That five women should come before all Israel to demand what no woman had a "right" to, the ownership of her patrimony, was unheard of!

The gathered assembly must have gasped at their reckless courage. Not only were they challenging Moses, they were daring to question what had been held up as divine law. It is to Moses' credit that he was willing to go back to God for clarification.

So it came to pass that when Moses brought the question to the Lord, "the Lord spoke to Moses, saying: 'The daughters of Zelophehad are right in what they are saying; you shall indeed let them possess an inheritance among their father's brothers and pass the inheritance of their father on to them'" (Num 27:6-7).

Filled with their intuition of the rightness of their cause and a passion for justice, the women carried forward in the strength of their solidarity. They made a change for the better for themselves and for the women who followed. (See, for example, Joshua 17:3-4.) Is there a healing lesson for us in this story?

Where do we see injustice? Surely it exists in the world at large. We can easily name the places and the causes. Sometimes it's less easy to see injustice in our immediate environment, however. We are so accustomed to societal injustice that we often just accept it as "the way things are." But remember the daughters of Zelophehad.

Is there justice in housing, in job opportunities, in the way certain classes of people are treated: the elderly, the poor, the physically challenged, the slow, the weak, the sick? If for one day we could escape from our cultural biases, we would see a host of wrongs in need of righting. But then what? What can we do about it?

We can band together and work for righteousness. No, one voice alone may not be sufficient. But a chorus of voices has a chance. We can step out in front of the assemblies of the 20th century and we can demand justice...and more! We can demand compassion. Side by side, hands held in unity, we can be victorious. Ours can be the "shout heard round the world."

Abigail: The Wise

Abigail was the wife of Nabal, a wealthy owner of sheep and goats in Carmel in Judah (cf. 1 Sam 25:2-42). David and his men were in the region and he sent messages to Nabal asking for contributions of food for himself and his army. In his request David reminded Nabal that when they had been in the region before, pursued by Saul and his men (1 Sam 23:14), they had left Nabal and his property unmolested. Indeed, "They were a wall to us both by night and by day, all the while [Nabal's men]...were with them keeping the sheep" (1 Sam 25:6).

But Nabal refused the request. In fact, he "shouted insults at them" (1 Sam 25:14). David was enraged and vowed revenge. So David and his men armed themselves and set off for Nabal's to kill every single male of his household. One of Abigail's servants informed her of all that had transpired and what was to come, and she immediately went about to right the wrong and to head off disaster. "Then Abigail hurried and took two hundred loaves, two skins of wine, five sheep ready dressed, five measures of parched grain, one hundred clusters of raisins, and two hundred cakes of figs" (1 Sam 25:18). Then, without telling Nabal, she set out for David's camp and intercepted him.

With quick wit and much wisdom, as well as intelligence and beauty (cf. 1 Sam 25:3), she turned aside David's wrath. She apologized for her husband, gave David the gifts she had brought, praised his virtue and goodness, warned him against the terrors of his own conscience should he shed innocent blood, and blessed him saying, "If anyone should rise up to pursue you and to seek your life, the life of my lord shall be bound in the bundle of the living under the care of the Lord your God; but the lives of your enemies he shall sling out as from the hollow of a sling" (1 Sam 25:29). Having received David's blessing in return, she went home again.

The story continues with the prompt and rather fortuitous death of Nabal and the equally prompt and, one assumes, fortuitous marriage of Abigail to David!

Abigail was a woman of wisdom who had managed to claim her own personal power. She stepped outside the role her culture had assigned her of obedient-at-all costs wife and made her own moral decision. She acted fearlessly and spoke wisely. She allowed her nurturing power to overcome cultural restrictions and, in so doing, warded off death and vengeance. Quite simply, she lived her truth.

The word "simply" here can disguise the demand that living the truth makes on us. Yet, if *we* are to be heroines, that is what we must do. We must listen to God dwelling in us and that insistent voice that says, "This is the right, the good, the holy thing to do." Then we must act on it. Such acting may not always be the easiest course, but it will be the most natural one. Doing the holy is always life-giving, and that's what we women are all about.

The Witch of Endor:
The Compassionate

I would like to mention one other woman, though her place in Scripture is obscure and even puzzling: the witch of Endor. The "important" part of the narrative surrounding her is not what makes her interesting to me, but rather the way in which she responded to suffering.

King Saul sought her out to tell his future. Through her, he found out that he was soon to die. He was literally prostrate with fear and hunger "for he had eaten nothing all day and all night" (1 Sam 28:20).

Despite the fact that witches had been banned by laws both human and divine, the author of Samuel makes her a kind of ancient "Glenda the Good." She is so moved by compassion at Saul's plight that she slaughters her calf, makes bread, and sees to it that Saul has nourishment. She may have been a messenger of death, but her woman's impulse was to preserve life.

The Healing

What strikes me in these stories, as well as in so many others about women in the Old Testament, is the model they offer of what God knows all women can be: brave and risk-taking, even in the face of death, in order to protect life. I don't believe that any of Scripture is an accident; so I think it is no accident that these women appear as they do, quietly proclaiming our vocation in their own way: to be heroines in bearing, giving and protecting life.

We need to spend time in prayer with and about these women, allowing our best selves to respond to them. As they become real for us, flesh and blood women who lived and loved and gave life, we will find that they challenge and encourage us to discover our own strengths and power. Making two hundred cakes of pressed figs to placate an angry warrior is probably not what our lives will call us to. Different ages demand different responses. But what about making two hundred loaves of bread to feed the hungry and the homeless? What about unleashing all that power in our imaginations, all the possibilities of our intuitions, all the joy of our playfulness for our families, our communities, our world?

We are a legion of heroines in the making. As we pray we will find God being born in us and we will be reborn as daughters of God and heroines in the birthing of a new creation.

Prayer

Great God, I thank you for inspiring men to write tales of the less spectacular women, of the women who quietly went about their task of being life-bearers. I thank you for the women mentioned here and others like

Rebekah and Rachel and Zipporah, and all the women who have been faithful to you and to their calling as women.

Remind me, gracious God, when I feel too small and insignificant to solve great problems, that, acting in your name and power, I can accomplish your most important mission for me: the preservation and nurturing of life. I know I will probably never do mighty deeds that catch the notice of the world. But I am grateful to know that even little things can affect the course of our history.

Give me the grace of courage to accompany my love of family. Grant me the strength to cherish life even when the *law* would take it. Let me always remember that those condemned to death also have the right to succor and nourishment for whatever life they still have left.

Send me sisters in the struggle for truth. Let us find together the good that you would have us do in your name.

All you holy women of the Old Testament, pray for me and for all women in every place and circumstance. Amen.

Chapter Six

Mary, Mother of God
The Unbroken Vessel of Holiness

Discovering Mary as a healing gift for women was a real revelation for me, though I suppose it's disgraceful for a well-brought-up woman, educated in Catholic schools, to admit that. Mary? The greatest woman who ever lived? Didn't the nuns always hold her up as the ultimate example? Yes, yes, and yes again. But somehow it just didn't "take."

I couldn't relate to Mary as she was taught. There she was: beautiful, a golden halo around her head, clothes always ironed and immaculate, every hair in place, pink plastic roses between her toes. Perhaps I need to be pardoned for saying so, but this image was certainly no woman I have ever encountered.

So I paid lip-service through the devotions the sisters prescribed. I said the rosary and sang the hymns. I was even "May Queen" once, crowning the Mary statue while all around me a couple of hundred children sang, "O Mary, We Crown Thee," and a dozen or so of my eighth grade female peers looked on with some degree or other of envy. That's all Mary was to me: a statue and no more. She was perfect, immaculate and hopelessly outside my experience or grasp.

It wasn't until many years later that God revealed his mother to me. It was a mighty, glorious and healing revelation. For I discovered a woman who was full of grace...and full of guts. She was not some pale and fragile being who floated around in a cloud of passive submissiveness. Far from it. Mary was a courageous woman, a gallant woman who met challenges, who seized life, who struggled with mystery and who—in the meeting, the seizing, the struggling—found her own holiness.

Mary was a woman, just as we are. Just for now, let's put aside our images of Mary as the Immaculate Conception, the Assumption, the Coronation, and the holy card pictures with halos and cherubs and pink plastic roses. Let's look at Mary's life as she lived it.

In a Town Called Nazareth

Even today Nazareth is nondescript. This dusty little town occupies a hillside not far from the Sea of Galilee. Mary may have been born and lived her childhood in this dusty, poor town. Remember, she was once a little girl who played with toys, imitated her mother's chores, delayed setting the dinner table as long as her friends were outside playing, and dreamed of getting married and having a home of her own.

That she was also very religious is not the extraordinary thing we would think it today. Her society was religious. Life was governed by the Law...and by the Romans. Prayer and attendance at the synagogue were taken for granted. No good Jew would have it any other way. Mary grew up in an age that longed for the Messiah, the anointed one who would set the people of Israel free.

So we have Mary, the good Jewish child, who became Mary, the adolescent, who suddenly found herself confronted with a choice that many of us would have run from. When we talk about the Annunciation now we have centuries of artists' renderings and poets' musings and theologians' reflectings to make it "real" for us. But all those representations are just that: a picture-perfect scene embroidered with piety and devotion that is most likely very far removed from what really happened.

But for the sake of argument, let's suppose that an angel who looks like all the holy cards really appeared right in front of her, with white wings and long golden curls. That angel said all the things just as Luke reported them: that Mary had found favor with God, that the power of the Most High would overshadow her, that she would conceive and bear a Son who would be called "Son of God," that he would rule over the house of Jacob forever, and that his kingdom would never end. All this would happen miraculously.

Would You Say "Yes"?

Wouldn't you trip all over yourself to say "yes"? Hold it. Don't commit yourself too quickly. Think about it for a moment from Mary's perspective, the time before B.C. and A.D. had been invented.

You are happily engaged and soon to be married. You live in a small town where nothing is secret for long. You have been offered the choice of whether or not to bear a "Son of God," which—in those days—was a phrase applied to any really holy man.

You are not living in nineteen-ninety-something with the resurrection an historic fact, when out-of-wedlock children are almost commonplace, when a discarded fiancé is only a minor inconvenience. Instead, you are living in a time when your fiancé could have you stoned for infidelity, when society did not look the other way at fatherless children, when "Son of God" as we understand it was not even a dream. Would you still say "yes"?

The Gallant Maiden

Mary did. Certainly she surrendered to the will of God, without doubt. But this young woman was also very brave, brave enough to accept a challenge and to grapple with the first of many mysteries that life had in store for her. Mary's "yes" shows incredible faith and incredible gallantry. We need to think more about what it meant to her and what it can mean to us.

She had to face parents, fiancé and neighbors. It couldn't have been easy. Though Scripture doesn't tell us how her parents reacted, we can guess. Even Joseph, who loved her deeply, thought of divorcing her. How Nazareth must have gossiped! Mary, betrothed, suddenly disappears from town to go visit her cousin and returns, months later, obviously pregnant. How difficult it must have been. But she did it.

What healing is there for us women in this part of the story? Perhaps it is the knowledge that we, too, can make hard choices, "weaker sex" though we be, and can live with the misunderstandings and hardships that those choices demand of us. We are made of the same stuff as Mary. We too can allow the Holy Spirit to overshadow us. We too can give birth to the Son of God in countless ways throughout our lives. "Behold, we are handmaids of the Lord. Let it be done to us and let us cooperate in the doing."

To Bethlehem

Now picture Mary, close to nine months pregnant, hearing that she and Joseph must go to Bethlehem for the census. Ever attentive to the voice of God, ever courageous, now greatly swollen with child, Mary made the long and difficult journey. She knew that in all likelihood she would have the baby before she could get home again. She knew that she would have her child in a strange place without her mother or sisters or aunts or anyone she knew close by to help her. She knew that she would have to draw deeply from her own inner strength and her deep faith. She acted with great courage.

Now, cut to Bethlehem. What do we find? Was it a neat, clean stable where the animals had all just been bathed and the straw was sweet and fresh? Did the angels hover everywhere while the shepherds came in, all rosy and clean, having been dressed by Central Casting? Was Mary veiled and robed in clothes just back from the cleaners, while Joseph looked on, leaning on his highly polished staff, looking rather removed from the entire scene? Ah, Christmas cards.

Yes, they're pretty, but they have denied the overwhelming mystery of the Incarnation. They have sapped Jesus, Mary and Joseph of their own humanity, leaving us with God-in-disguise, wonder woman, and ineffectual husband. Could any woman who has ever delivered a child, even in the warm and sanitary confines of a hospital, relate to this Mary?

So let's back up just a bit and try to glimpse what things were more probably like, to get a better perspective on the birth of Jesus. Can you imagine going into labor on the street and being told that there is no warm and relatively private place for you to have your baby? How would you feel when the pains grow stronger and closer together while you and your husband wander from place to place, only to have the doors shut firmly on your mounting panic? What would it be like to take refuge in an animal stable because the baby is coming and there is no time or place left to look for another shelter?

Stables, even well kept ones, are not immaculate. Farm animals smell. Shepherds, among the lowest ranks of that society, were neither clean nor tidy. Having a baby is an exhausting and difficult and painful process. Of course, we don't have the details, but my hunch is that poor Joseph—religious taboos notwithstanding—was probably the reluctant midwife.

What a woman Mary was! Little girls may be made of "sugar and spice and everything nice" as the old nursery rhyme says, but they're also apparently made out of steel and grit and granite, if Mary is any example.

I've seen one picture of the nativity that has always struck me as being somewhat closer to the truth than the crib scenes we have in church. In this picture Mary is lying down, rather wan and exhausted, one hand reaching down toward the manger where the newborn is. Joseph stands by looking nervous and anxious, but protective and proud. They radiate happiness, and it is a human happiness we can believe in and experience in our lives. Mary is a woman who has survived quite an ordeal. We can believe in her too.

When we are feeling homeless or alone, when we are frightened at some coming event over which we have no control, when we are in pain, Mary of Bethlehem comforts and confronts us. She did it with God's help. So can we.

Only the Beginning

The birth of the child was only the beginning of the story. The stay in Bethlehem must have been at least forty days in order that Mary might go up to the Temple for her purification. Did the little family live in the stable that whole time? Possibly, since they weren't wealthy. Or perhaps they went to stay with Elizabeth and Zechariah who lived close by. Can't you imagine the two babies, John and Jesus, lying close to one another, being played with together, and beginning their fascinating and intertwined destinies even in the cradle?

At any rate, the time came for the purification of Mary and the presentation of Jesus in the Temple. We all know the story of Simeon and Anna. But have we ever taken time to think of what these encounters must have meant to Mary?

How wonderful Simeon's first words would have seemed to her, what confirmation that her child was indeed quite special, "destined for the falling and the rising of many in Israel" (Lk 2:34). But then came his warning, "A sword will pierce your own soul too" (Lk 2:35). Surely the young Mary must have felt some fright at such a prophecy.

The Flight from Herod

Where they were staying and at what point we do not know for certain. What is certain is that Joseph was warned of danger to the child and told to take him and Mary to Egypt. Scripture tells us that Joseph rose immediately and "by night" they began their flight from Herod into Egypt.

Think of what this must have been like for Mary. As the crow flies—and crows are definitely not donkeys contending with mountains and desert—it is about two hundred miles from Jerusalem to Egypt. At best the journey takes ten days and probably many more. This journey was with a small baby, very little money and no welcoming family at the end of it.

It was a journey into the unknown. It was the journey of a refugee family, hurrying from terror to a strange land where people spoke a different language, where there was no job waiting, where nothing was safe, secure or familiar. Granted Joseph had a marketable trade; and granted too, there was a large Jewish population in Egypt among whom they might have settled. But it was still hard and unfamiliar and frightening.

Take strength from this Mary when you are called to take a strange and difficult road to an unknown destination. This Mary, this woman, did it with God's help. So can we all.

Back to Nazareth

Historians could certainly make a reasonably accurate guess at how long the holy family stayed in Egypt, because we are told that they returned to Nazareth after the death of Herod. Most say that Jesus was somewhere between three and six years old at that time. Regardless of exactly when it was, however, they did return. Then Scripture is silent except for the story of Jesus preaching in the Temple at the ripe old age of twelve. Many years pass in obscurity, years that were spent in Nazareth. We can only guess at what Mary's life was like. What was she about, this woman who is now called the greatest of all women? What heroic tasks were hers? What great deeds did she do that have won her so much honor and respect? Was she rich, "successful," famous? Did she demand that all Galilee and Judea take note of her Son? Not at all.

Mary was a housewife, a blue-collar housewife, who cooked and cleaned and mended and picked up after her husband and child, who brought water from the well, who talked and laughed with the other women of Nazareth, and who dreamed wonderful dreams for her child. In short, she was a wife and mother. She simply did what she was called to do: to make a home for her family. It was in the doing of these simple and unglamorous tasks that she was made great.

She must have spent a lot of time, too, watching her Son and waiting for some sign of the amazing things foretold by the angel, by Simeon and Anna, some indication of the destiny of a Messiah. She must have wondered at his ordinary humanness. She must have been mystified when he seemed to settle down to the life of a Nazorean carpenter like Joseph before him. Where, when, how would all the prophecies be fulfilled? Was she wrong? Was he really only a man like any other? When would he begin to be about the business of saving Israel?

Frequently women speak of their disappointment in their children, how the children showed such promise and then, for whatever reason, seemed to settle back into mediocrity or worse. In times such as those, we can only remember Mary and what she must have felt for so long. Pray to her. She understands. She too had a child; she too had to watch and wait helplessly for what God would ultimately do. She had to let go of her own expectations. But she never lost faith in God or in her child, even when it seemed that some terrible mistake had been made at Calvary. She never lost faith, this simple housewife, this ordinary woman hidden away in a tiny village in Galilee.

She Believed

Once Jesus' public ministry began, things didn't improve too much. True, his gifts began to be manifested.

He healed, he blessed, he even raised from the dead. But he had so many enemies. Rome still stood firmly on the heart of Israel. His friends...how could he hope to change the world with this motley crew of fishermen, farmers, tax collectors? Yet Mary believed.

Finally it came to the cross. This woman stood beneath it, watching the lifeblood of her child spill out on the ground, hearing his moans and cries and prayers. Did some remembrance of the angel's first visit come to her? "You will conceive in your womb and bear a Son, and you will name him Jesus. He will be great, and will be called the Son of the Most High, and the Lord God will give to him the throne of his ancestor David. He will reign over the house of Jacob forever, and of his kingdom there will be no end" (Lk 1:31-33).

If that were true, if she had not imagined it all, how could it have come to this? But she did not waver. She stood there, some part of herself dying with him. We can only guess at her bewilderment and pain.

The Strength of the Cross

Standing there on Calvary, Mary reflects an often overlooked aspect of women's spirituality: its strength, its ability to endure. She is an exemplar for all the women through the ages who have stood at the cross, however that cross appears, and brought the world and the Church through some of its darkest hours.

While wars were fought and "heroes" were proclaimed, the Marys at home made certain there was a home to return to. In quiet ways, these women have gone about their daily tasks while power politics in Church and state raged about and above them. They kept their homes intact when they could and, when even that became impossible, they took their children, their faith and their courage to a new landscape to begin again.

Mary has taught us. Black American women have learned from her as have the women of Central and South America, China and Africa. We may not be the ones named in the history books, but our strength at the foot of the cross is one of the greatest blessings of our womanhood. Mary endured. We endure. Our women's hearts say "yes" and know her presence as we take our place beside her.

Women: Myth and Reality

History has told us that women are somehow lesser creatures. But we can all fly in the face of that fiction with a greater truth. We can do it because of Mary. She showed us time after time what being a woman really is. It is being a chalice of life, ready to be filled with the seed of the Spirit, eager to give birth to the Son of God. You and I are still called to be chalices, to give birth to the Son of God.

A great Dominican mystic lived several hundred years ago whose name was Meister Eckhart. He preached all sorts of holy and worthwhile things, but in the midst of his life and preaching, one particular saying leaps out to challenge us all. It was something he said about Mary, and about us.

"What good is it to me that Mary gave birth to Jesus in her place and time, if I do not also give birth to Jesus in my place and in my time?"

And further: "We are all meant to be mothers of God, for God is always needing to be born."

While this call is meant for all people, men as well as women, it is particularly good for us to remember. We, after all, have been designed by God specifically for child-bearing and child-birthing. We are chalices to receive the seed.

Says Eckhart: "Whatever can be truly expressed in its proper meaning must emerge from inside a person and pass through the inner form." We must accept the seed deep within us if we are to give birth.

We are meant to give life to the Word, as Mary was, no matter the ungainliness of the pregnancy, no matter the risk, no matter the misunderstanding and perhaps even the sneers of others. We follow her example, refusing to consider self-protection or, worse, self-enrichment, if those stand in the way of life.

Christ-bearing is hard and difficult. It challenges our culture. It is not a job for the timid or weak or even the temperate who might also be called "lukewarm." Christ-bearing is compassionate, but it is a compassion that does not compromise truth. It is hearing the angel, in whatever guise that angel comes, and saying yes. Christ-bearing is stepping out into the darkness and discovering that we have become the light.

Just as Christ-bearing is courageous, Christ-birthing is nearly outrageous. It sometimes means homelessness and poverty. It means receiving, even welcoming, those who have nothing. It means being able to hear about angels from the unlikeliest people, and still being able to believe and find God at work in it all. It may even mean dirt floors and animal dung, strange places and unfamiliar accents. It may mean having doors slammed in our faces and the embarrassment of having to allow the birthing because the time has come even though the circumstances are not the most providential possible. It means labor pains and even blood.

No, Christ-birthing is not an easy thing. But it is our call, and for us women it is our grace. As Mary leads, so we must follow. We too must be women blessed, the wombs of our doing and saying and living filled with the fruit of

God, ripening in prayer until it is ready to be born, nourishment for a hungry world.

A Mary Story

I share the following story with you for a number of reasons. In our time, abortion is stealing life from thousands of children and joy from thousands of mothers. Given the statistics, it is almost certain that some of you reading this book have had an abortion and many more of you know someone who has had one. I include this story because, regardless of what any of the "experts" say, women who have had abortions sooner or later pay a terrible price. They must be healed and we must pray for them.

One woman who had had an abortion many years ago came to see me for healing prayer. Somehow the enormity of what she had done had finally dawned on her, and she was writhing spiritually in grief and guilt. She'd been to confession but was still not free of depression and dark dreams. She had killed her child. Nothing could change that, but she was seeking some kind of release from the terrible burden she felt.

We began to pray together and, as we prayed, I had a "vision" of Mary caring for those thousands of babies, playing with them, laughing with them, and mothering them until their own mothers finally came "home" to claim them. I shared that image with the woman, and it was a miracle to see what happened.

In a deep recess of her heart she felt that the child had been abandoned to some sort of lonely place, not of earth but not quite of heaven either. Somehow the idea of Mary taking care of her child gave her peace. We continued to pray. I suggested to her that she might like to name the baby and then, very specifically, give the child to Mary.

She did that and we prayed on. A very real change came over her. She had been released from the guilt and the paralysis which that brings, and she was at peace in her relationship with her child. Mary, the gracious mother, had once more brought the healing power of her Son to a wounded woman and given her rest from her torment.

Healing in Jesus Through Mary

If we are searching for our healing, there is no one better than Mary to point the way. Remember Cana. Apparently it was Mary, out of all the guests, who was first aware that the wine was gone. Mary was most attentive to the needs of hospitality. It was Mary who went to Jesus and then, despite his reply, from the deep part of herself where lived her faith and courage, said to the servants, "Do whatever he tells you" (Jn 2:5).

Do whatever he tells you...and the miracle will happen. For what does Jesus tell us at Cana, at Capernaum, at Nazareth, at Jerusalem, at Calvary? Jesus' instruction is simple. Fill the urn with water and I will take it from there. Let the chalice accept the seed. Allow the vessel that is yourself to be filled with love and only see what I will do for you.

Love, woman. Love God. Love your neighbor. Love yourself. Love as I have loved you.

Do whatever he tells you. Do love, not valentines. Do love that is as "strong as death" (Sgs 8:6). Do love that is "patient...kind...not self-seeking" (1 Cor 13:4-7). Do love that heals and gives life. Do love that is not afraid to name evil. Do love that can halt the Pharisees in their tracks and—for the great love of God—throw the money changers out of the Temple. Do love. Birth Jesus. Do whatever he tells you.

Mary shows us the swiftest path to healing. If we are uncertain, she will take us by the hand and lead us to her Son, who is the Way and Truth and Life.

Go to Mary

Mary is a woman, born of woman, daughter of earth, Mother of God, now Queen of Heaven. She is not out of reach, not a statue. She is real. She is a mother, a sister, a friend, a companion, a woman who lived and felt all that we live and feel, a woman of greatness who did nothing great as the world defines it. She didn't go through life with all the answers, nor did she have a guarantee of what was to be. But she lived the questions with courage, strength, resourcefulness, endurance, humility and womanliness.

She was a woman, just as you and I are women. She did what she had to do at each moment and believed always that Yahweh would somehow take her small offering and turn it into something more. She was right. He did.

Mary understands all the pains and hurts and graces and blessings of being a woman. I believe that she not only stands ready, but reaches out to us to lift us to her Son that we may be healed to discover God's dream for us, the dream he has had for us from the very beginning, the dream of healed and holy womanhood.

Prayer

O God, how is it possible to thank you enough for the great gift of Mary of Nazareth? Yet I want to thank you. I want to praise you for her creation. I want to shout my gratitude that she is part of our history, and I want to glory in the fact of her womanhood.

How can I thank you Lord? By being like her. But I need your help for that. So I ask you now, for myself and for all women, that you grace us with her graces, bless us with her blessings, fill us with the seed of your Spirit as you filled her.

Make me pregnant with your Son. Let me carry that sacred fruit within me always. Help me to give birth to him. No matter the cost of the bearing and the birthing, keep me ever faithful to that holy task.

Thank you for making me a woman, a chalice for life. Let me live true to that great calling.

Mary, mother, sister, friend, pray for me and with me. Lead me to your Son. Amen.

Chapter Seven

Elizabeth
Partner in God's Plan

Some days we wonder who, if anyone, is really in control. Everything seems chaotic, our prayers seem to be ignored, and it appears that God has gone on a holiday. Those days challenge and test us. But on those days we can also thank God for having given us the woman Elizabeth.

Scripture says little about her, but what it does say is rich in detail and meaning. We know that her husband was a priest, so we can conclude that she enjoyed not only a higher social rank than did her cousin Mary, but she probably also had more of this world's goods. Elizabeth would have had good clothes and plenty to eat and a house that was larger than most and well kept. What she didn't have, and what she wanted desperately, was a child.

As we have noted before, to be barren in Israel was to suffer more than just a personal loss. It was to endure society's view of that condition as well which considered barrenness a great tragedy and assumed it to be a punishment from God.

How Do We Respond?

How many of us, denied the one thing we feel we need to be happy, become bitter and resentful toward God? Our human natι ⸱e always seems to want more and to blame God if prayer is not "answered." But Elizabeth was not like that. According to what we read in Luke, she and Zechariah were "righteous before God, living blamelessly according to all the commandments and regulations of the Lord" (Lk 1:6). Despite their disappointment that the "plan" they must have had when they were first married had gone awry, they persisted in their belief in the Lord's love and goodness. "My thoughts are not your thoughts, nor are your ways my ways, says the Lord" (Is 55:8). They trusted, even in their disappointment. They were willing to let go of their plan in order that the Lord's plan—whatever that might be—would be carried out.

And so it was. Long past child-bearing years, Elizabeth suddenly conceived a child, an extraordinary child with a special place in God's plan for the salvation of the world.

The Healing Lessons of Elizabeth

This story holds many healing lessons. The first and most obvious one has to do with trust, for the Lord's ways are *not* our ways, for which we can gratefully say, "Thank God!" We have all known people, indeed, we can probably number ourselves among them, who are quite content to do the will of God provided we can tell God just what that will is. When something interferes with our carefully structured "will," we get angry and sometimes even turn our backs on God. After all, who knows better than we what we need and what will make us happy? Then

Elizabeth speaks to us gently, "No. Remain righteous; remain faithful to God because he knows what is best for you and will do it."

God is good. We say that so often that it almost stops having any real meaning. But we need to say it every day and we need to believe it. God does not do evil. In those times of chaos when we're wondering who, if anyone, is in control, we can remember and believe what we so often say: God is good. Then we can act on that belief and remain in prayer, in righteousness and trust that he will bring good about as long as our hearts are in tune with his.

When evil happens, and it will, it is easy to blame God. Children are hurt by adults. Wars happen. Terrorists blow up airplanes. Accidents leave people crippled. The list could go on and on. So we question, "How come, God? Why did you make this happen?"

The Truth about Evil—and about Freedom

The truth is that God didn't make it happen. People made it happen, people who listen to the enemy instead of to the Spirit, people who are careless or deliberately sinful or caught in the grip of some awful addiction. People do evil, not God. Then why doesn't God do something about it?

God gave us free will, a mighty and terrible gift. He gave us the ability to say "yes" to him. He also gave us the equal ability to say "no," because he loves us and he wants us to love him back: freely, not because we have to but because we want to. Then it's up to us to choose the blessing or the curse, the death or the life, just as it says in Deuteronomy:

Surely, this commandment that I am commanding you today is not too hard for you, nor is it too far away. It is not in heaven, that you should say, "Who will go up to heaven for us, and get it for us so that we may hear it and observe it?" Neither is it beyond the sea, that you should say, "Who will cross to the other side of the sea for us, and get it for us so that we may hear it and observe it?" No, the word is very near to you; it is in your mouth and in your heart for you to observe.

I call heaven and earth to witness against you today that I have set before you life and death, blessings and curses. Choose life so that you and your descendants may live, loving the Lord your God, obeying him, and holding fast to him; for that means life to you and length of days, so that you may live in the land that the Lord swore to give to your ancestors, to Abraham, to Isaac, and to Jacob (Deut 30:11-14, 19-20).

God Is There

When evil happens, know that God is there. But know also that each of us has been given the power to choose what we will do—without divine interference. God whispers and begs and sometimes even thunders, but he will not do more than love us into changing our hearts and our ways. He has given the gift. Being God, he will not take it back.

The Visitation

The story of the Visitation is easy to love. It is the mystery of the rosary which I urge all of us to pray for our own mothers each day. We place our mothers with Mary and Elizabeth and pray for their healing and for the healing of any bad memories in ourselves or our siblings which might spring from the time we were in the womb. We ask that our mothers might become aware of their own blessedness as women, as mothers, chosen by God for their own stories, just as surely as Mary and Elizabeth were.

We see Mary and Elizabeth, one very young and one not young at all, coming together in joy at the new lives that are forming in their wombs. Their mutual rejoicing is so good, so holy. They are caring for each other and for their children in the most powerful way of all: by giving thanks to God for the gift of life.

In this era of casual abortion, Elizabeth can be a powerful intercessor and a great healing example for women who are considering such a "solution" to an unwanted or "inconvenient" pregnancy.

In this light the story of Elizabeth and her child has another special message for us. That message has to do with God's plan. Yes, I believe that God has a plan, though please don't ask me for specifics. In this we must be like Elizabeth, praying and wondering and hoping. We can't pretend to know the mind of God any more than Elizabeth could. But God does have a plan. Elizabeth would appear to be one shining example of that plan in action.

She had wanted a child for years. But her child, as all children, had a particular place in God's plan. When God knew the time was right, she conceived. God wanted John. He wanted him at a particular time and place, just as God wants each one of us...at a particular time and place.

God Wants You

How many of us have been told that we were "unplanned," "accidental," or even "unwanted"? Maybe—in human terms—that is true. We were told that we certainly were an unplanned, even an unwelcome surprise. Even if we could even understand the inconvenience, it still hurt to be told about it. It hurts to know that, given a choice, your mother or your father or both would not have given you life.

It hurts too when either or both of them obviously prefer another sibling. I think women, prey to "it's only a girl," are particularly vulnerable to this pain. How many times have we heard other women say, "My parents wanted a boy"? or "As soon as my brother was born, I fell out of the picture"? Unwanted, unplanned, "incorrectly" gendered, we ache.

The good news, the great news, my sisters, is that God wants you. God wants you so much that he designed you from all eternity—you with your mixed bag of gifts and graces...and garbage. "From the womb before time" he begot you. He calls you by name. You are his (cf. Is 43:1).

Unplanned? Unwanted? Not by any maneuvering of the imagination. God has planned you, planned for you, very carefully from all eternity because God needs you. You are part of the plan, or, quite simply, you wouldn't be here. He needs you in your own uniqueness. You have something to do for the building of the kingdom. You are special, chosen, called. You are wanted beyond your most daring dreams. God wants you! This is the greatest call and consolation in all the world.

Certainly, some parts of the plan are more obvious than others: Mary, Elizabeth, John, Augustine, Gandhi, Mother Teresa are just a few who come to mind. But no part is more necessary. We have a place. We have a mission. What more healing grace is there than to know God's desperate need for us? What more beautiful destiny than, like Elizabeth, to bow gracefully to that need?

If we, as she, remain in righteousness and use our free will to obey the voice of God, we need never fear that we are failing to carry out our piece of the divine plan.

Exalting the Christ-Bearer

Elizabeth did one more very powerful and healing act in the story of the Visitation: she recognized and even exalted the Christ-bearer who was her cousin.

"Blessed are you among women," she cried, "and blessed is the fruit of your womb" (Lk 1:42). How wonderful those words must have sounded in Mary's ears as she was affirmed and confirmed in her obedience to God. How wonderful those or similar words would sound in the ears of the other women who come into our lives.

As we noted in the last chapter, being a Christ-bearer is difficult and often thankless. Elizabeth knew that instinctively. She knew that Mary, simply another human woman, needed her blessing, her encouragement. What a great and holy example that is for us.

Let us give affirmation to the Christ-bearers we meet, those who quicken the life within us and bring us into intimate contact with Jesus. Let us bless them in their mission and be eager to let them know that we feel and appreciate their goodness. Let us accept with joy the blessing of their presence. Above all, let us pray for their perseverance in bringing the saving Word to a saddened world.

Prayer

Holy Jesus, I thank you for Elizabeth. I thank you for her example of patience and righteousness even in disappointment and trial. I thank you for her own blessedness among women and for the holy fruit of her womb.

I ask, Lord, that you would grant me the grace to be faithful to you no matter the trial or stress; to continue to believe in your goodness and great care for me even when it seems to be otherwise.

I thank you for the gift of my life and the knowledge that you need me, that I am part of your plan for the world, that I am wanted, desired and loved by you in ways I cannot even begin to imagine. I thank you, Lord, for all the graces of my existence.

Let me always recognize you as you are brought to me by others. Remind me, please, to bless and thank those who have brought you.

Elizabeth, I ask you to pray for me and, in a special way, for all the pregnant women of the world. Amen.

Chapter Eight

The Woman at the Well
A Case of Co-Dependence

Jesus loves to heal us from our wounds into the fullness of our womanhood. Few stories illustrate this better than the story of the woman at the well, another nameless but not unknown woman, who was healed in an unexpected encounter with Jesus (cf. Jn 4:4-42).

The very fact that Jesus spoke to her amazed his disciples, for according to the Jewish custom of the time, no man ever spoke to a strange woman in public. But he saw her hurt, her wound, and could not resist speaking to her, loving her as she was, and loving her too much to leave her as she was.

Her story, as it is told in John, uncovers one fact for us quite clearly: co-dependence, while it has only been named in our time, is an ancient illness. The woman at the well is indeed a classic case of that dysfunctional and debilitating disease. It's a disease that can and does afflict people of both sexes, but—probably because of the way we are trained—it seems to strike hardest at Christian women.

What Is Co-Dependence?

Before we go on with the story, however, let's move away from that sun-drenched well in Samaria in order to try to explain what co-dependence is and why we are so subject to it. Having said that, however, I realize that there is no one absolute definition of co-dependence. Perhaps that's because it is hard to define what is not, and that's exactly what a co-dependent woman is: a *not*. She is *not* truth, *not* reality about her own image, wants, needs and feelings. She lacks any sense of herself and lives only by other people's definitions of who and what she is. She is like an empty chalkboard who allows those who have an impact on her life to write on her and tell her who she is. When a relationship ends, the board is erased and she waits passively for the next person to come along and define her.

Her whole identity comes from outside herself. She has no center, no core self from which to live. She is defined by the roles she must take on: wife, mother, teacher, corporate executive, vowed religious. She plays out those roles in whatever way is necessary to please the other. That other may be husband, boss, religious superior, best friend, child, or a host of other possibilities. Who the "object" of her need is, is not the issue. The co-dependent person is caught in an unreal world, an unhealthy relationship, because the object is what gives the woman her security and the very definition of her existence.

She has no self-esteem, but gathers all her esteem from other people and from other things: her husband's success, her children's grades, her clothes, her education, her job performance, her ability to fill someone else's needs. She does not believe in her own unique precious-ness, in her intrinsic worth just because she is. She is lost to herself and ultimately very lonely. She is incapable of independent existence.

The co-dependent woman does not act. She reacts. If the object is in a good mood, then she is in a good mood. If the object is in a bad mood, then she must fix it for she assumes she is the cause. While she may look generous and giving, she is engaged in one of the most selfish stances in the world because she is really all about control. "You must be happy because when you are happy that means you love me, and you must love me. I will do anything and be anything to make you love me."

Not Me!

Well, you say, that doesn't apply to me. I hope you're right. But if you are right, then you're also exceptional. Experts say that about 95% of us operate at least part of the time, if not most of the time, out of a co-dependent posture. So if you want to give yourself a quick test on whether or not you act co-dependently, ask yourself how often you say "no."

Whether, like the woman at the well, it's a case of five husbands and a live-in lover or, like most of us, it's five committees and a "perfect" marriage, or five community obligations and a parish ministry, it's all the same. The co-dependent woman cannot say "no."

Then Why Do We Say "Yes"?

Why do we say "yes" when we're already tired, over-burdened, short-tempered and feeling put upon? Is it because we're good Christians, or because we are flaming co-dependents? From the outside they may look a lot alike, but inside they are worlds apart.

A Christian first loves herself and then loves her neighbor in the same way. A co-dependent has no self from which to love. Instead, she tries to buy love, earn love or coerce love from another. A Christian serves a need. A co-dependent needs to serve. A Christian acts out of compassion. A co-dependent reacts out of compulsion. A Christian is centered on God. A co-dependent is centered on the other, the object. A Christian prays for miracles. A co-dependent expects to perform them.*

Aren't women, especially Christian women, encouraged into this bent-over posture—the "devoted" mother, the "uncomplaining" wife, the "long suffering" religious, the woman of whatever age or race or education or social position who will always "do anything for you"? Isn't this the model woman, the "perfect" Christian: sweet, never complaining, never angry, always available?

No! Christians are followers of Jesus Christ, who complained about the apostles' thick-headedness, who called the Pharisees some awful names, who got angry, who wept, who allowed people to be themselves, and who withdrew from the crowds and claimed some time for himself to rest and to pray. Jesus did not hesitate to serve when there was a need. Jesus also did not hesitate to take care of himself, recognizing his own needs. It is only the co-dependent, not the Christian, who will insist on washing clean feet.

Co-dependent women are everywhere on the outside and nowhere on the inside. Their identities come from their doing, not their being. So their endless repetitive cycle continues its frantic spiral of containment, control, pleasing, yes-ing, until...one day we come to draw water at the well and our lives are changed forever.

---

* For much of the comparison between Christian and co-dependent behavior, I am grateful to Dr. Marie Gatza of Cor Ministries, Paoli, PA.

At the Well

> So he [Jesus] came to a Samaritan city called Sychar,
> near the plot of ground that Jacob had given to his
> son Joseph. Jacob's well was there, and Jesus, tired
> out by his journey, was sitting by the well. It was
> about noon. A Samaritan woman came to draw
> water, and Jesus said to her, "Give me a drink." (His
> disciples had gone to the city to buy food.) The
> Samaritan woman said to him, "How is it that you, a
> Jew, ask a drink of me, a woman of Samaria?" (Jews
> do not share things in common with Samaritans.)
> (Jn 4:5-9)

It is easy to spot this woman's wound immediately.
Jesus asks for water. But rather than giving him a straight
answer, or just simply handing him a cup, she replies in a
flirtatious way. Jesus has already "broken the code" by
speaking to her. Now she wants to see if she can draw him
further into their casual and unlikely relationship. Does
he find her attractive? Is that why he spoke to her? Is she
"worthy" of his further attention?

She knows only one way of relating to a man and that
is sexually. When we learn her history, we find that she is a
woman who has, indeed, spent a lifetime in unhealthy
relationships—five husbands and now a live-in lover! (cf.
Jn 4:17-18). She is a woman who can only identify herself
in terms of male relationships. How she came to be so
wounded we do not know. But the woman, the person,
has been lost. She does not know herself and she has
surrendered her essence in order to be "loved" by a tragic
succession of men.

She has been lost. Only Jesus can find her.

How true this is of the co-dependent woman who is
out of touch with her own feelings, her own needs, her

own truth. She lives instead for others or for one other; everything else is sacrificed to preserve those relationships. She will give up all—friends, family, health, anything—to hold on to "love." For she does not love herself and only receives her worth from the outside.

Confronting the Truth

In Samaria that day, the woman looked at Jesus and waited to see her reflection in his response. What a shock it must have been when, rather than the distorted reflections she had seen all her life, Jesus—who will not be drawn into unhealthy relationships—confronted her with her own truth.

That's the first thing that must be done to recover from co-dependency: to confront the truth. The more painful and uncomfortable it is, the more desperately we need it. The pain and discomfort indicate our denial and our fear. Where will our shadows go if someone tears down the screen on which they are reflected? Where, indeed? The light of truth scatters shadows and leaves no screens behind which to hide. It leaves only the reality of who we are...in the sight of Jesus Christ.

It's terrifying for the co-dependent woman to step out from the shadows. "If they really see me, they cannot love me." But come forward, sister, for the reflection you will see in the eyes of Jesus will comfort you even as it challenges you. You are lovable just because you *are.* You can neither earn nor buy real love. All your suppression of yourself will not get you love. All the outside compliments will not give you self-esteem. All the good deeds in the world will not help you to stand straight before God.

Let Jesus speak the truth about yourself to you as he did to the woman at the well. Acknowledge that truth.

Then let him speak the truth about himself to you. "Those who drink of the water that I will give them will never be thirsty. The water that I will give will become in them a spring of water gushing up to eternal life" (Jn 4:14).

The water Jesus offers is love, real love, healing love. When we drink his life-giving water we no longer thirst for an identity; we have it. As we drink of it more and more, we discover our own self-worth where it has been all along—in ourselves as beloved of God.

It's Not Easy, but It Is Possible

I don't want to oversimplify and make healing sound easy. Recovery from co-dependency is a long difficult process, which is often quite painful.

The people who were previously the objects of our compulsion, for instance, will probably not be grateful for our recovery, any more than were the Samaritan woman's townspeople. She had brought them the good news of the Messiah and of her own release from captivity. But they could hardly wait to try to bring her down again, to belittle her, to bring her back to her former state of being a nobody. "They said to the woman, 'It is no longer because of what you said that we believe, for we have heard for ourselves, and we know that this is truly the Savior of the world'" (Jn 4:42). Perhaps they knew it, but they obviously still didn't quite get it!

Why try to take away her moment of importance if they did not feel threatened by this new, free, powerful woman among them? Very often as the recovering co-dependent woman begins to rise, to stretch, to live her own truth, those who used to "love" her (or loved to use her) will turn away. But what kind of love demands obeisance and captivity? What kind of love demands that the loved one be "less than"? Certainly not the love we receive from those life-giving waters.

So though it will be hard at times, don't falter. Your recovery will never be lonely, for Jesus will be with you every step of the way, offering cup after cup of water from his well, healing you, making you whole.

Love Yourself

As we begin to respond to ourselves, to discover ourselves, Jesus will reveal to us more and more of his truth. He begins our healing and then invites us to discover the healer, the Messiah, the anointed one. "I am he, the one who is speaking to you" (Jn 4:26). The healer has come to offer us life and to free us from our compulsions. Love your neighbor, yes, but first know and love Jesus and yourself.

The woman at the well may seem like a distant story, but it holds a profound meaning for us. Jesus still comes to us wherever we are: making beds, washing dishes, rushing to get our errands done, carpooling, in our offices, our boardrooms, our living rooms. Wherever we are, he is there too, and he wants to heal us. He knows our woundedness, our bentness, our need to be loved. He is patient with us, even when we try to cajole him away from the truth.

Be Healed

Jesus offers each of us "life-giving waters," the truth of ourselves and of him. He stays in conversation with us while we tackle the difficult task of confronting those truths. Honest self-assessment is difficult. But Jesus is there, gently offering himself as balm for the hurt, as water to wash away the suffering. I know. I've been there. Like that nameless Samaritan woman of long ago, I cannot help but share with you and anyone who will listen that this healer is the Messiah, the Savior of the world.

Prayer

Thank you, Jesus. You told us that you are the living water, that you are the way, the truth, and the life. I ask you to wash me now in those waters and reveal to me all the truth that you would have me know about myself and you.

I want to honor my Creator by honoring myself: this woman who was brought forth in love from the heart of God. Please, show me that self, that real self, and teach me to love and trust her. Take away my nagging guilt and shame, so that I may see the truth of who I really am in the eyes of God. Let me know my own worth as a daughter of God and let me give praise to God in acknowledging that worth and living it.

I desire to honor the Holy Spirit by living in the freedom from captivity that the Spirit offers. Please help me to break the chains of co-dependence on others and grace me to dance freely in the breath of your Spirit. I long to delight in being myself and all that I can be.

I yearn to live in truth. So heal me, loving Jesus, of everything in me that is not truth. I wish to know and to glory in your truth. I want to claim my life in truth and to live it in the way you set out for me, not in neediness but in love.

Thank you for your encounter with the Samaritan woman. Thank you for loving her into health. Thank you for leaving the story behind to offer hope and healing to me and to all of us who have lived so much of our lives uncentered and focused only on the other.

You are, indeed, life-giving waters; and I come now to drink deeply, never to thirst again.

Holy woman of Samaria, pray for me and for all of us who have not yet discovered our deepest and truest selves. Amen.

Chapter Nine

Mary and Martha
Choosing the Better Parts

Mary and Martha were two sisters who lived in a small town near Jerusalem. Jesus came to visit them one day and, in the course of just a few hours, set them both free to discover the truth of their womanhood. Though Scripture only tells us a small part of the story, we can imagine a bit about what the rest was like. That may be a bit presumptuous, but somehow I don't think Jesus will mind.

The scriptural part of the story goes like this:

> Now as they went on their way, he entered a certain village, where a woman named Martha welcomed him into her home. She had a sister named Mary, who sat at the Lord's feet and listened to what he was saying. But Martha was distracted by her many tasks; so she came to him and asked, "Lord, do you not care that my sister has left me to do all the work by myself? Tell her then to help me." But the Lord answered her, "Martha, Martha, you are worried and distracted by many things; there is need of only

GO IN PEACE

one thing. Mary has chosen the better part, which
will not be taken away from her" (Lk 10:38-42).

For years and years many of us have stood staunchly
on Martha's side. After all, how thrilled would Jesus have
been if there hadn't been any supper? We remember our
childhood holidays when fathers, uncles and brothers
gathered around the football game while mothers, aunts
and sisters went wild pulling out the good dishes and the
holiday table linens. We all know the scenario. Isn't that
the lot of women, to take care of the feeding while the
men do whatever it is they prefer to do?

The answer is no! We'll see that if we really listen to
Jesus in this story and look behind the few recorded lines
to discover what it's all about. So let's do that. Let's imagine how the scene unfolded. After Jesus spoke to Martha,
what happened next? Suppose the story continued something like this....

"But, Lord," said Martha, "aren't you hungry? If I
don't see to this supper there will be nothing at all for you
or any of your friends to eat."

Jesus looked at her with great love, then turned to
Mary said, "Let's both go into the kitchen to help her. We
can include her in our conversation while we get the
supper ready." He told Martha, "We don't need an ex-
travagant meal. Something simple will be fine and then
we will have enough to share with the beggars who sit not
far from here by the well."

So Jesus and Mary went into the kitchen and mixed
and chopped and stirred and did with Martha whatever
else was necessary to prepare the supper. While they did
these things, Jesus continued to speak to them about the
kingdom of God and how, in preparing and sharing a
meal, they were participating in building that kingdom.

"The kingdom of God," he said to them, "is like a table set out in the open and laden with fresh breads and hearty wines. The table is available to all who wish to eat. But some walk by, too concerned with the riches of their own tables to want to settle for bread and wine. Some pass by, so involved in their business pursuits that they don't even see what is being offered. Some are suspicious of anything offered for 'free.' But some stop, smell the delicious aroma of the new bread, notice the rich red of the wine, and take time to refresh themselves, giving thanks to God for those gifts so generously offered and shared."

In short order the supper was ready and they sat down to eat. By that time Lazarus was home from his errands in Jerusalem and he joined them. As he ate, he noticed some subtle change in his sisters, but he couldn't quite put his finger on what had happened. They were the same, but they were also different.

Whatever it was, they were happier. Martha seemed more peaceful. And Mary? Mary helped to clear the table when they had finished and then went in to help Martha clean up. Something certainly had changed. Then he glanced over at Jesus and smiled. Of course! Wherever the Master went changes occurred. Why should this house be any different?

The Healing Power of Jesus

Three people were healed that afternoon: Mary, Martha and Lazarus, though at the point at which we left the story they still didn't realize all the implications. Jesus healed the image of what women are and so set them free to be. It could only have happened because of who women are and who Jesus was: a man not afraid to do "womanly" things—like helping in the kitchen. He was a man who brought about justice and who cared very much about being "inclusive."

Martha

Martha was healed, obviously, as Jesus pointed out to her the "better part." He wasn't suggesting that the tasks of keeping up a household were a waste or something that should be neglected altogether. He would have been denying his own mother's vocation had he done that. Nor was Jesus blind to the necessities of housework. What he did point out to Martha, however, was that any task—be it cooking or cleaning or selling stocks or manufacturing computers or teaching CCD—could become "lesser" if it interferes with our relationship with him.

In a way, this can be a story of healing for everyone, not only women. But we should take advantage of the healing fact that Martha was a woman and apply it to ourselves. Jesus freed Martha from the expectations of her society: that she be confined to household tasks. Jesus said to her, "One thing only is needed," and that is to remember that our first "task" is to be in relationship with him.

Mary

Mary was healed of the same kind of expectation, though in a different manner. In the Jewish world of Jesus' time it was the prerogative of men to study theology, to "sit at the feet" of the wisdom of God and to learn. The very presence of Jesus was enough to free Mary from the limits that her culture would have put on her. There certainly were limits! A popular teaching at that time was "Rather should the words of the Torah be burned than entrusted to a woman." Jesus obviously did not believe this, nor—in the freedom that he gave her—did Mary.

Freed to Be Women

Jesus gave great freedom to both women, just as he offers freedom to us. He taught them, showing them that stereotypes can chain us. Through word and deed he broke through what society had told them they must be to allow them to discover themselves as God had created them. Though none of us may have been taught exactly as Mary and Martha had been, the healing and the lesson are the same.

In the company of Jesus we may discover who we truly are, not only who we have been told we are. Whether we are systems analysts or housewives, whether we belong to churches that acknowledge the gifts and equality of women or not, God has created us to be whole persons. We are capable and we are called. The struggle may be long and difficult, as we find we must contend with the powerful. But in the presence of Jesus and in his power, we can be victorious.

Imagine how Lazarus must have felt. After that day with Jesus it's quite possible his sisters sometimes invited him to share in some of their tasks. He must have seen new dimensions in both of them as they shared their duties and as they each made time to pray and contemplate the words Jesus had spoken to them. Perhaps too they set a simpler table...and perhaps the beggars of Bethany no longer went hungry.

Jesus was a man who fed others: his followers, his listeners, the five thousand, we who now come hungry to his table for the Eucharist. Women are usually the ones who feed. Let us be healed into feeding the multitudes of the hungry as well.

Building the Kingdom

If we can accept this imagining of what might have happened on that sunny afternoon in Bethany, then we can also draw another healing conclusion. In giving the example of himself as participating in the preparation of the meal, Jesus pointed out to Mary that building the kingdom requires work as well as listening, activity as well as stillness.

We know from our own experiences that sitting at the feet of Jesus and letting the rest of the world go by is a most delightful way of being. Retreats, for example, are a special and precious time when we are graced to sit in absolute quiet at his feet. But Mary and Martha, before their healing that day, were two halves of a whole; and so I—in searching out my vocation as the particular woman I am—have found my wholeness in the Dominicans. One of the guiding rules of the Order of Preachers, the formal name for the Dominicans, is to contemplate and to share with others the fruits of that contemplation.

Contemplation is necessary—our Mary side. Equally necessary for us is that we share the fruit of that contemplation in preaching, writing, mopping the floor, cooking dinner, or whatever work the Lord presents to our hands, work which also includes praying. We healed Marthas find our place in apostolic work while the healed Marys in the cloister work through intercession.

One in Womanhood

Mary and Martha healed were one in their womanhood, though still two separate people. If we are to be healed, then we need to pay close attention to this particular story. It is so easy for us to be caught up in our work that we neglect the very energizing source from which our work must flow, the source whose name is Jesus. All work and no prayer can make Martha a barren woman, one who cannot produce real fruit for the kingdom. A branch disconnected from the vine can bear no fruit, and we have Jesus' own word for that. "Just as the branch cannot bear fruit by itself unless it abides in the vine, neither can you unless you abide in me" (Jn 15:4).

Contemplation without sharing the fruit of that contemplation is another kind of sterility. The "better part" is meant to be life-giving. Any other use of it is selfish and contradicts the life and message of Jesus.

You Are the Son of God

Though Martha has been much maligned over the centuries, we can rejoice with her whenever we remember that it was she, not Mary, who proclaimed the Lordship of Jesus.

Think about the story of the raising of Lazarus from the dead (cf. Jn 11). We tend to focus so totally on the miracle of that resurrection that we may overlook some of the smaller miracles that are told as well. For instance, if we stop and listen to her, we can see how well and truly Martha was healed.

As Jesus arrived in Bethany, having heard that Lazarus was ill, it was Martha—wonderfully true to her character— who came rushing out to meet him. She didn't wait for him to come to the house. He probably wasn't even quite to Bethany yet. But Martha, the energetic assertive doer, jumped up, ran out the door and down the road before anyone quite knew what she was doing.

Having been mildly reproachful with Jesus, "Lord, if you had been here, my brother would not have died," she goes on to express her belief in him. "But even now I know that God will give you whatever you ask of him" (Jn 11:22). Then after a short exchange with Jesus about resurrection and what that means, Martha proclaimed the hymn of her faith, the hymn of our faith, the hymn of all Christians everywhere.

"Yes, Lord, I believe that you are the Messiah, the Son of God, the one coming into the world" (Jn 11:27). Perhaps, despite his sorrow at the death of Lazarus, Jesus smiled at this show of faith.

The Result of Contemplation

The Martha we met in Luke's earlier story might never have said this because, quite simply, she might not have known it. But since that blessed day, Martha had been spending time "at the feet" of the Master, figuratively as well as literally. Out of this contemplative stance she had come to believe, to know that this man Jesus is, indeed, the Son of God.

It's obvious that Martha's character had not changed. She was still outspoken and quick to act. She had not become Mary. She had not denied the truth of herself or attempted to submerge herself into another personality. She was still adamantly and gracefully Martha.

It's equally obvious that her whole approach to life within that character had altered remarkably. One who never contemplated, who never took time for prayer and reflection, would never have come to know Jesus for who he was. Martha had been healed in a wonderful way. Jesus offers this healing to us too.

One Advantage of Being a Woman

Through the years religion has often come to be seen as the territory of women. It is unfortunate because many men have become merely signers of collection checks. That is a loss for them and for all of us. We need the richness of the both/and. It is another sad triumph of expectations.

The good news is that since religion is "ours," as long as we don't try to claim much administrative or policy-making power, we are free to become Mary-Marthas without drawing any criticism down on ourselves. We are free to participate in lay ministry, to pray, to contemplate, to be compassionate and passionate in the service of God. That is good news.

We are free to invite our families to prayer. We are free to encourage, even to insist on Christian values in our workplaces, whether in or out of our homes. We are free to proclaim the Lordship of Jesus. That is great freedom indeed.

Like Martha and Jesus, we can be concerned with feeding the hungry in our neighborhoods and in our world. As we spend time with Jesus in prayer, he will teach us ways in which that hunger can be appeased, both the hunger of the stomach and the hunger of the soul.

Let us be healed then in his power and immense love. Let us be healed to be women who bring people to feast at the table he invites us to spread with the food of his compassion and ours.

Prayer

Loving Jesus, thank you for Mary and Martha. Thank you for the Mary and Martha in me, and thank you for showing me the way to healing in my life through their lives. Thank you for giving me the desire to listen to you and then to act on your word. Thank you for inviting me to listen. Thank you for acting with me and through me.

Too often I am so concerned with doing and accomplishing that I forget just being with you. Yet I know that you are the real source and power of all the things that I do or accomplish. Help me to remember that, Lord, and please, help me to remember that without you there is really nothing I can do that is worthwhile.

I ask also that you increase my faith in you, Son of God, Messiah. Let me believe in you so strongly that miracles great and small are done in your name. Especially now I ask for the miracle of food. I know we have food in abundance, food that rots away uneaten, food that is wasted without thought. The miracle of food I ask, Lord, is really the miracle of the human heart, that we will be graced to share and to find ever more creative ways in which to do that sharing so that no one in the world goes hungry.

May I also bear the food of your word to all whom I meet, the word that I hear as I sit like Mary at your feet. Give me the grace to speak that word no matter how difficult it might be for me.

Jesus, may I always be fed at your table and, in the blessing of my womanhood, bring others to feed there as well.

Mary and Martha, pray for me and for the hungry. Amen.

Chapter Ten

Talitha Koum

Little Girl, Get Up

Childhood has great delights. Chief among them, perhaps, is the absence of responsibility, that bug-bear that drags us down and makes us feel burdened. So it is tempting to pretend at being children, and I use the word "pretend" deliberately.

The distinction between being the kind of child God wants me to be and the kind of person who only "pretends" at childhood is a large one. The first invites me to be the sort of child that Jesus called to himself, the child I must be in order to enter the kingdom of God. Then there is the other kind. Let's elaborate a bit on that distinction and then go on to the story of Jairus' daughter.

What Is It to Be a Child?

What are children? Certainly they are not just short adults. They have different attributes and different ways of seeing the world and engaging in life. They have not yet been taught all the limitations. They have not yet become completely bound in expectations. They are spontaneous. They are creative. They are players, not workers. They are intuitive and loving. In particular, they are dependent, which may be the most important word of all for our discussion here.

They are absolutely and totally dependent. Not only that, they are perfectly comfortable in that dependence. Their dependence is not co-dependence; their dependence is reality.

But aren't all our urgings toward independence? From the time we first learn to say "no," don't we want to be our own persons, released from parental restraints? Isn't "dependent" generally a "lesser than" term? Why should we be encouraged to stay dependent?

First, think for a minute of a baby, any baby, holding that baby, cradling it in your arms. Think of that baby's absolute dependence on you for everything: shelter, food, a clean diaper. That baby can't do or accomplish anything on its own. It needs you for its very survival. Even more, it doesn't mind the dependence. It accepts it and may even enjoy it, if it thinks of it at all, as part of how things are. You are everything to that baby and that's okay with the baby, absolutely okay.

Second, think of Adam and Eve in the garden, which was Paradise as long as they honored their dependence on their Creator but which became something other than Paradise the minute they cried, "No. We will do things our way, not yours." That misguided thrust for independence cost them greatly. Now, think again of the baby.

Listen to Jesus

Listen to the words of Jesus: "Truly I tell you, unless you change and become like children, you will never enter the kingdom of heaven" (Mt 18:3). Prayer has led me to believe that what Jesus was talking about here was dependence, complete and total dependence on God and acceptance of that dependence without question. He calls us to depend on God just like a baby depends on its parents, for that is our reality. We are totally dependent on God, though we often live in denial of that fact. Without God we are nothing; we do not even exist. We are as helpless in the arms of God as babies. We need God for everything. As we come to know that, to believe it, and to live out of it, we become what we are called to be: children of God. Our entrance into the kingdom depends on that.

The Pretend Child

To pretend to be a child is something quite different. To pretend to be a child is to take upon oneself a role and to use it as an excuse to be any number of unattractive things. We all know women who go through life pretending to be children. They may use baby voices and sometimes even baby talk to cajole others into thinking of them as children because there is safety in that, safety from responsibility. But nothing could be farther from what Jesus really wants from us and for us.

Let's turn to Scripture now to find Jesus' desire for us.

Jairus' Daughter

According to Mark 5:21-43, Jairus was a synagogue official. Because his daughter was dying, he came to Jesus, who agreed to go to Jairus' house. As they were on their way, they were interrupted by a woman who touched Jesus and was cured of a hemorrhage. We'll return to that "interruption" later.

Jesus continued with Jairus and a large crowd of followers, only to be met by people bearing the awful news that the daughter had died. We can understand Jairus' agony, and we are told that at the house everyone was weeping and wailing. But Jesus went among them and proclaimed that the child was not dead but sleeping. Then, to their great astonishment, he went in to the child, took her by the hand, and said, *"Talitha koum,"* "Little girl, get up."

Is it only coincidence that the child was "about twelve" (Mk 5:42), that age which usually coincides with puberty and the beginning of menses? Is it an accident that she was at the age between childhood and womanhood? I don't think so, at least not in God's plan, because why else was her age even mentioned?

In the great and wonderful movie *Jesus of Nazareth,* the child sits up at Jesus' command and leans toward him. That scene portrays what the Gospel message is to us.

"Get up and be about becoming a woman. Be a little girl no longer. Be everything instead that your womanhood calls you to be: life-giving, compassionate, creative, expressive, intuitive, loving...and dependent on me. In this way you will be a woman while remaining the child my Father longs for you to be. Accept the responsibility of womanhood. Cherish the dependence of childhood. Little girl, get up."

So Jesus calls to us even at this moment. He calls us to get up from our beds of immaturity and to accept the great and responsible vocation we have as women. He wants us to live, not to die; he wants us to live in the glory of his healing. He wants us to participate as adults in the building of the kingdom, and he wants us to enter that kingdom as dependent children of the Father.

It's not hard to be an adult, despite what Peter Pan

would have us think, if, in our adulthood, we remember our total dependence as daughters of God.

Some Ignatian Wisdom

St. Ignatius of Loyola offers some very sound advice for those of us who desire to be children of God. He says this: in time of difficulty or question, we should reverse the order in which we usually do things. Our normal and very human inclination is to look to ourselves for a solution first, then perhaps to meditate on some similar situation in the life of Jesus for an example, and then—and only then—to pray.

Turn that upside down—or right side up—says Ignatius. Pray first. Meditate on the example of Jesus second. The odds are, having done that, you'll never have to fall back on yourself alone for resolutions.

Pray first. Acknowledge your dependence. Let God show you the way to the most salvific activity. Let God tell you what your womanhood demands. Let God be first. God will take care of what's second and third.

Jesus calls us to be real children, not pretend ones, at the same time that he tells us to "get up" and be women. It's not as contradictory as it sounds, especially if we can keep in mind the child/woman of this story.

The Woman with the Hemorrhage

This almost parenthetical healing story in Mark nearly parallels the healing of Jairus' daughter and deserves some close attention. This time we meet an adult woman whose womanhood, her lifegiving and life-bearing potential, had gone haywire. Her hemorrhage would have prevented her ability to conceive, making her barren. In ancient Israel this was considered a terrible fate, and it made her ritually unclean.

She was an outcast, literally an untouchable, for according to the law in Leviticus, "If a woman has a discharge of blood for many days, not at the time of her impurity, or if she has a discharge beyond the time of her impurity, all the days of the discharge she shall continue in uncleanness; as in the days of her impurity, she shall be unclean. Every bed on which she lies during all the days of her discharge shall be treated as the bed of her impurity; and everything on which she sits shall be unclean, as in the uncleanness of her impurity. Whoever touches these things shall be unclean, and shall wash his clothes, and bathe in water, and be unclean until the evening" (Lev 15:25-27).

Her fertility denied, the woman of the Gospel suffered the denial of her womanhood by her society as well. She had sought relief from many doctors, spending all she had in her search for healing. Ignatius might have said that she had been trying to find the solution in her own way. Then she heard about the new healer in town: Jesus of Nazareth. Graced with the grace of dependence, she crawled toward him.

See her now moving toward him through the great crowd, edging her way bit by bit, knowing that if she could even touch only his cloak she would be healed. Feel her pain as those who saw her leaped aside lest they become "unclean" by brushing against her. But still she persisted in her wounded womanhood and her graced childhood, seeking healing. On she came until she touched him. "Immediately her hemorrhage stopped, and she felt in her body that she was healed of her disease" (Mk 5:29). Jesus was instantly aware that something had happened.

"'Who touched my clothes?'... But the woman, knowing what had happened to her, came in fear and trembling, fell down before him, and told him the whole truth" (Mk 5:30, 33).

Jesus said to her, "Daughter, your faith has made you well; go in peace" (Mk 5:34).

Go in Peace

In so many ways and by so many people, our womanhood has been wounded too, by society and by ourselves. Yet Jesus wants to heal us and he will heal us, if we will only accept the responsibilities of adult women and the dependence of female children. No, it's not a coincidence that these two healing stories are so intertwined. In both cases Jesus enables women to be women, and he wants the same for us if only we will heed our double call to dependent freedom.

Our Participation in the Healing

Another interesting parallel can be noted here concerning an occurrence in both the stories of the little girl and the raising of Lazarus. It seems to be an integral part of helping people out of their tombs and back into a healed life, which is the point of this book.

Once Jesus had raised Lazarus, he turned to the crowd and said, "Unbind him and let him go" (Jn 11:44). Once the little girl had been raised, Jesus said that she should be given something to eat (cf. Mk 5:43). These are small details, but they seem to carry an important message for us.

Jesus heals. Only Jesus heals. There is no question about that. He calls us forth into the fullness of our womanhood. But he knows that healing does not stop there.

He knows that we need each other to continue, encourage, untie and "feed" the life he has given. He knows that we can, in him, be healing for one another.

It is not enough that we are healed if we do not offer the way to that same gift and consolation to our sisters and brothers, if we hug it selfishly, rejoicing in our own lives but failing to do what we can to work with Jesus to bring life to all who need it. Jesus has given us, quite clearly, an important and specific work to do. We are to untie each other as he breaks open our tombs. We are to give each other something to eat, an historically female occupation, so that our new lives will be sustained. Remembering Cana, we are to love as we are loved.

Prayer

Lord Jesus, I thank you for the healing you gave to the little girl, the daughter of Jairus, the same healing you offer me. I thank you for healing the woman with the hemorrhage just as you heal me into the full potential of my being.

I thank you for that adult womanhood, for that part of me that gives life. I thank you for teaching me about the necessity of my dependence on you.

I know that you love me, so I ask in total faith that you heal me too. Heal me of pretense and of fear of responsibility. Heal me of the wounds others have inflicted on me because I am a woman. Heal me of any lingering feelings of "uncleanness" I might have because of attitudes about my menstrual cycle. Heal me, dear Jesus, and let me be healing for others.

Remind me that I must always untie and feed those whom you would free. Help me to remember, too, that I am needed in your great work on this earth. Thank you for calling me to get up and to go in peace. I pray that I may always be faithful to that call.

Unnamed women of this story, pray for me and for all my sisters that we may be life for one another. Amen.

Chapter Eleven

Mary Magdalene
The Healing Ways Women Pray

Prayer is a powerful healing tool. Because woman's prayer is different from man's prayer, just as women are different from men, this chapter will focus on prayer. It will highlight someone who at first glance might seem to be a most unlikely subject for that focus: the woman known to us as Mary Magdalene.

Why Mary Magdalene? She never actually appears "praying" in Scripture. Why not Mary, the mother of Jesus? Why not Hannah or Miriam, Elizabeth or one of those women whose prayers are documented in our faith history?

Why Mary Magdalene? Because she is like us. Probably neither you nor I have ever prayed anything as poetic as the Magnificat. Sometimes we don't even know how to pray. More probably, we don't even realize that we are praying, which makes us very like the Magdalene, very like her indeed.

I also chose her because it is my experience as I work and travel with and among women that the majority of us identify with Mary Magdalene. Not that we are a population of reformed prostitutes!* But most of us carry at least a remnant of the "guilty of being a woman" disease and at some level we feel responsible for most of the world's evils since time began. So we identify with the Magdalene, and perhaps rightly so. She was a survivor...and it was prayer, the healing prayer of her life, that made survival possible.

Our Woundedness

Most of us experience three major wounded areas in our lives with which the Magdalene can help us: our patterns, our priorities and our perspectives. They are healed, as all things are healed, through prayer in the presence of Jesus. As we pray, our patterns, perspectives and priorities fall into line. We become healed women, just as Mary Magdalene did.

Patterns

We have to imagine Mary Magdalene's first encounter with Jesus, because Scripture is silent on that subject. Mark (16:9) tells us that Jesus cast seven devils out of her which could well have led to her famous conversion. But even that says nothing about how she first met him.

Surely she had heard about Jesus. Magdala was a small town on the Sea of Galilee which Jesus must have passed. His reputation was such that she could hardly have avoided hearing about him. But then one day....

---

* It is important to note that only in the Western Church have we defined the Magdalene as a "fallen" woman. The Eastern Church has a very different tradition. It says that she was a wealthy woman who chose to follow Christ and who used her wealth to help spread his message, especially following the resurrection. It is believed that she even went to Rome to try to convert the Emperor.

She Speaks

I can still remember what I was wearing: a dress the color of the lake on a spring day. The cloth was a gift from a caravan owner I knew and, though I was going nowhere special, it was one of those days when I just felt like looking beautiful. So I put it on, musing as I did that it would give the women of the town just one more thing to whisper about at the well. I was shameless, brazen, bold. I would not dress in boring homespun colors nor creep around corners furtively with my eyes down. But I wander from my story.

As I walked into the market square, I noticed a crowd gathered around a man who seemed to be speaking to them, though I wasn't close enough to hear his voice. Ah, I thought, it must be that man from Nazareth I've heard so much about—the magician so good that he makes even the Egyptians seem second rate. They say he performs all kinds of wonderful tricks.

I was curious enough, and confident enough in my new dress, to go a little closer, not caring what I might have to endure from the mouths of the "good" people of Magdala, many of whom certainly knew the path to my door! I wanted to see what was holding the crowd so still around him.

So I went closer and closer. Then it was too late, because as I came nearer people began to pull away from me. He looked up to see what was causing the stir among his listeners. He looked up. He looked at me. I was lost. No, I mean that I was found. Oh, I'm still not sure how to say it.

He looked at *me*—not at my dress or my hips or the pull of cloth over my breasts. He didn't see the dark paint on my lashes. He only saw me, Mary of Magdala. He saw me! Suddenly, for the first time in my life, I felt good about myself. I began to realize who I am and what my being a woman is really all about....

The Look of Jesus

Now the Magdalene had certainly been looked at by men before, too many men, too many looks. Those were looks of raw lust, looks that made her an object, looks of contempt, looks of shame. She was accustomed to such looks and she knew how to deal with them.

But how could she deal with the look of Jesus? This look recognized her soul and loved her. He simply loved her. Love was outside her experience, but not outside her understanding. It was an experience she had long ago stopped dreaming of. But...if love could be possible...what then?

Her pattern was broken, the pattern that all her adult life and probably much of her childhood had said that she was an object, something to be used for the pleasure of others and then discarded, the pattern that made her nothing at all—nothing beautiful, nothing worth caring for, and certainly nothing holy.

This pattern said that sex was power for her, a way to control and to get what she wanted. It was a pattern of degradation into which all the pieces of her life were fitted.

In the look of Jesus all that was changed. She saw herself cherished for herself and she felt her dignity. Suddenly she knew what being a woman was really all about.

That, my sisters, is a healing prayer, a healing moment, when we realize why we are women and how we are women and whose women we are. Such was the experience of the Magdalene on encountering Jesus. His look loved her as she was and invited her to be so much more.

Looking at Jesus is a prayer. Letting Jesus look at us is a prayer. Asking him to know us better and to help us to know ourselves better is a prayer. Letting him into every single room of our secret interior houses, welcoming him and celebrating his presence there is a prayer. In that prayer we will discover the glorious truth of who we are, of our womanhood, the truth that for too long has been covered over in looks that regard us as objects. The pattern of the ages will have been broken and our freedom will begin.

Priorities

In Luke (7:36-50) we read the famous story of Jesus dining with the Pharisees when Mary Magdalene came in. She is not actually named, but tradition holds that it was she. She came to anoint Jesus, to wash his feet with her tears of repentance, and to dry those tears with her hair. What a fantastic healing prayer!

Perhaps she got dressed up for the occasion. Knowing that her healing had only begun, it's probably safe to guess that she did. Old habits will cling even in their brokenness. For such a long time her only identity had been in her appearance, and it was hard to lay that aside, even as she knew at some level that her physical appearance was unimportant to this man. However, she did come as herself.

She didn't pretend to be other than who she was and she came in spite of what anyone else was going to think or say or do. She was determined to get to Jesus.

Imagine that you hear that Jesus is going to have dinner with the bishop. You hear it and you want to be with Jesus. Can you imagine in your wildest dreams crashing the bishop's residence? Barging past the locked doors and the attending priests? Brushing past all the people who would say, "What on earth is she doing here"? Just to get to Jesus?

Mary Magdalene did it. She wanted to be with him so much that she just didn't care who was standing in the way. Nor did she care how much struggling she had to do to get there. She didn't care about what anyone did or said or thought. She had to get to Jesus. She had her priority. He was worth whatever struggle was necessary.

How often have we struggled to pray? We feel as if we're not making contact, that all kinds of obstacles separate us from Jesus. We feel as if we are in a "dry" space and that we are boxing with shadows, as it were, in our frantic attempts to get close to him.

Take a lesson from Mary Magdalene. She got to Jesus in spite of all the obstacles. She got to him and she stayed. Needless to say, the Pharisees were not at all amused, as the Pharisees are still not amused when women struggle through their carefully guarded ranks to get to Jesus. They wondered aloud why Jesus would allow such a woman to come near him and to touch him. What did Jesus say?

"Then turning toward the woman, he said to Simon, 'Do you see this woman? I entered your house; you gave me no water for my feet, but she has bathed my feet with her tears and dried them with her hair. You gave me no kiss, but from the time I came in she has not stopped kissing my feet. You did not anoint my head with oil, but she has anointed my feet with ointment'" (Lk 7:44-46).

Jesus recognized her love, the love that was offered in the way women very often offer their love: in passion and emotion, in service and hospitality. He recognized that love and blessed it. He knew that to the Magdalene he was the priority, the only one whom she really loved in the world.

We too may break open our jars of ointment, all

those gifts which God has given us, despite what the world or the culture or the churches might say to us. Despite what they might attempt to deny us, the example of the Magdalene shines through two thousand years of history and says to us, "Pour out your ointment in his service and know that he loves and wants it even if the Pharisees cannot accept it. Don't let the threat of their power stop you, woman. You are gifted for his service and, if you will only make him your priority, your gift cannot be undone nor the power of your tears ignored."

Jesus forgave her sins as she knelt there weeping, acknowledging his Lordship in every action she performed. That's a good way to start a prayer: to repent of those things in our lives that are in need of repentance and to acknowledge that Jesus and only Jesus is Lord of our lives. He is Lord of our womanhood and it is safe in his hands.

How safe? Let's listen to him again. "Her sins, which were many, have been forgiven; hence she has shown great love. But the one to whom little is forgiven, loves little" (Lk 7:47). The great blessing of love, human as well as divine, is unconditional forgiveness. Jesus taught that to Mary Magdalene, and we pray he will teach it to us as well.

Perspectives

Luke 8:1-3 is a short passage about some of the people who traveled with Jesus. One of them was the Magdalene, who walked with him through each day, watched the miracles and heard him speak. Jesus became the source and center of her life.

This says much about prayer. Mary Magdalen was constantly aware of Jesus' presence, and what is prayer but that? It means being aware that no matter where we are, no matter what we are doing, no matter how we are feeling, Jesus is present. We can't hide from him. We can't get rid of him. He is always with us, always.

In remaining aware of him at each moment and in each task of our day, we turn our lives into a prayer. In offering him our sleep at night, even those moments of unconsciousness can become a time of prayer.

As Mary traveled with Jesus, she must have learned a great deal from him about prayer. She must have prayed for him. Don't we all pray for the people we love? She noticed when he got tired and when he was hungry. Because she loved him, she tried to help him in those moments. Doesn't God still depend on us to help him? We are his arms and legs in the world today. In that we are like Mary Magdalene in the prayer of her life, her following of Jesus, joining him on the road no matter where it went and being constantly attentive to his presence.

In this attentiveness we, as she, will gain a new perspective. When we open ourselves to the Lord and make our hearts available to him, he does the most amazing things! Sometimes he even lets us see the way he sees, and that is most assuredly a new perspective. We see ourselves and others in a new light, a light that enables us to love ourselves and others as God does: outside the tomb of expectations and in the freedom of his children.

At the Cross

We find Mary Magdalene once more at the cross. That is also a lesson in prayer. When almost everyone else ran away, who stayed? Mary of Magdala stayed, because she had learned to love so completely that she was willing to accept the pain of being there to watch the Jesus she loved die. She accepted what came, even the fact of the cross.

We have no immortal words from her lips on that occasion. She was probably crying too hard to speak. But as she knelt there at the bleeding feet of her Lord and heard him ask forgiveness for those who had crucified him, she must have learned something else about prayer. With her heart so in tune with his, she was able to join him in that prayer. She, who had been forgiven much, was taught the greatest forgiveness.

Our double gifts of passion and compassion, surrendered in prayer to the Lord of our lives, must lead us to pray for forgiveness of others, even to pray for our enemies. "But I say to you, love your enemies and pray for those who persecute you" (Mt 5:44). "Bless those who curse you, pray for those who abuse you" (Lk 6:28). In doing so we will discover an extraordinary and unsuspected blessing for ourselves. As we pray for our enemies, we find that they are no longer enemies, for it is impossible to remain angry at those for whom we pray.

The Magdalene also teaches us about forgiving ourselves, something we usually find at least as difficult, if not more difficult, than forgiving others. The Lord forgave her and she was humble enough to accept that forgiveness and to forgive herself. Otherwise she would not have dared to go with him on his travels or to kneel at the foot of his cross. She had to be able to say, "It's over; it's finished; it's behind me; it is no more. I have a new pattern now. I have new priorities and a new perspective. I am forgiven. I am loved."

If you find yourself stuck in old guilts, caught by the remembrance of old sins now forgiven, ask Mary Magdalene to intercede for you. She understands and will pray for you. "Much is forgiven those who love much."

In the Garden

The last prayer lesson we may learn from the Magdalene is found in chapter 20 of John's Gospel. "Early on the first day of the week, while it was still dark, Mary Magdalene came to the tomb and saw that the stone had been removed from the tomb. So she ran and went to Simon Peter and the other disciple, the one whom Jesus loved, and said to them, 'They have taken the Lord out of the tomb, and we do not know where they have laid him.' Then Peter and the other disciple set out and went toward the tomb" (Jn 20:1-3).

As the story goes on, we learn that the disciples saw that Jesus was gone and then they left to go back to Jerusalem. Why? We can't be certain. We only know that they did leave—but not this passionate, emotional woman. She stayed, weeping, beside the tomb.

"They said to her, 'Woman, why are you weeping?' She said to them, 'They have taken away my Lord, and I do not know where they have laid him'" (Jn 20:13).

Now stop and imagine yourself in that garden. It's a lovely spring dawn with the sun just a wish away and you're walking in the garden. The flowers are breathing fragrance out into the air. Your feet are just a little bit wet because the dew is still on the grass, and you are Mary Magdalene on your way to the tomb.

Only two days before you stood at the foot of the cross and watched while the life of the only person who ever loved you, whom you ever truly loved, dripped away. His body wracked with pain, he had suffered horribly. You too had suffered painfully. Now you've come to the garden and it seems almost a cruel joke to be in the middle of such a lovely dawn when all you can do is go to a tomb because the one you love is dead.

You're bringing ointment and you can't help but remember the first time you brought ointment for him, the first time you actually touched him. Now the ointment is for his dead body. Perhaps you will find comfort in this last small womanly service to your beloved.

You get to the tomb...and the stone has been rolled away! How can that be? Was someone there before you? You look and you look again and, yes, the stone is gone. You run those last few yards to see what happened. When you look into the tomb, you see that Jesus is gone! Someone has taken him away. Instead of Jesus you see two people there whom you've never seen before, and all they want to know is why you are weeping....

Magdalene says, "Why am I weeping? Why am I weeping? Because the body of the Jesus I love has been taken away and I don't know where they've put him. I pray to get that body back. That's all I want, that's all, God. Give me back that broken, dead body so that I can anoint it and know that, even though there's nothing left for me, I will have done what I could.

"So I'm crying. I'm crying so hard that I can't see. My vision is totally distorted with tears. Someone else comes in front of me and he, too, asks, 'Woman, why are you weeping?' Everybody wants to know why I'm crying! Isn't it obvious? I tell him, 'Sir, if you are the one who carried him off, can you tell me where you've laid him?'"

All I Want

How many times have I prayed for something, begged God to grant my request and cried so hard for what I wanted that I couldn't see what was standing right in front of me? That's the great healing lesson of the Magdalene, so intent on what she was asking for—a broken, dead body—that she couldn't see what God had given her: a risen Lord!

How many times have I been so fixed on what I was asking for, knowing what I wanted, knowing what I needed, that I was unable to recognize what God had given me instead? How many times have I heard others say that they had prayed and prayed for something but God didn't answer their prayer?

God *always* answers our prayers, but we are often too blinded by the tears of our own desire to recognize the gift that has been given. We ask for a body; he gives us a risen Lord. Time after time, he gives us infinitely more than what we ask for, or what we can even imagine to ask for. He is a giver of endless gifts, but we must sometimes dry the tears of our own desire, however good it may seem to be, in order to see what he is offering us.

If we can stay in touch with that truth, then we can run out of that garden with the Magdalene to proclaim to anyone who will listen, "I have seen the Lord!" (Jn 20:18). Let the tomb guards huddle in fear. The gift of the vision was given to a woman who loved more than she feared. The passionate, imaginative ability to love is one of the most blessed gifts of our womanhood. It was in love that Mary Magdalene discovered new patterns, priorities and perspectives. It was in love that she became the first to preach the Good News.

Along with her we may learn the heart of woman's prayer and find healing. Love is the greatest pathway to healing, love given and love received. It is our gift.

Prayer

Jesus, I thank you for touching Mary Magdalene and for inspiring others to write about her. I thank you for the love she gave to you, and I thank you for giving me that possibility.

Grace me with love, Jesus. Fill me with passion for you and for all your people. Let me learn from you new patterns for my being, new perspectives for my vision, new priorities for my life. Teach me to pray with my lips, my heart, and my entire nature. Let each beat of my heart be a prayer. Let each breath I breathe be a prayer. Let me creep as close to you as I can. Give me the courage not to care what others may think or say.

Fill me with the truth of your goodness and give me the faith to believe that all my prayers are answered in ways that will bring me ever closer to you and your Father in the power of the Spirit.

Let me go from the garden of each new morning to proclaim with my voice and my life that I have seen you, have heard you, have touched you, and that you are Lord.

Mary Magdalene, pray for me and teach me to pray with you. Amen.

Chapter Twelve

Women Healed and Holy
Other Encounters with Jesus

The temptation, of course, is to write several more individual chapters for each of the women to come here and some others who haven't been mentioned at all. But it's spring outside my window. The tree that so generously gives me welcome shade in the summer is budding green and each day the sun arrives just a little earlier to accompany my morning prayer. So I am lured away from the typewriter by warm days even as I am tempted toward it by the thought of sharing with you some final women's stories. If I am brief, then, please understand and think of me in the sunshine.

The Canaanite Woman

One of the charges leveled against women is that we are "nags," that when our minds are made up we simply will not take "no" for an answer. That always brings to mind the story of the Canaanite woman and her meeting with Jesus. While real nagging is certainly not a lovely trait in anyone, sometimes it's good that we won't take "no" without a protest.

As the story is told in Scripture (cf. Mt 15:21-28), this woman appears and calls out to Jesus to heal her daughter. Jesus ignores her completely. Then the disciples plead with him to send her away because she's been irritating them with her constant calling out. So Jesus replies by telling the woman that his mission is only to the Israelites.

At this point most of us would have gone away disappointed, even cowed. But not our heroine. Instead she persists in asking for his help. Again Jesus refuses, even comparing her to a dog. "It is not fair to take the children's food and throw it to the dogs" (v. 26). Accepting the label, she refuses to give up. "Even the dogs eat the crumbs that fall from their masters' table" (v. 27).

Jesus must then have looked up at her at last, startled, perhaps a bit amused, but definitely attentive. He sees her faith and knows that it is what has given her the courage to keep at him despite his disinterest. He says to her: "Great is your faith! Let it be done for you as you wish" (v. 28). Then he healed her daughter.

Often we are dismissed out of hand as unimportant because we are women. Frequently what we say is ignored or labeled "illogical." The healing message of Jesus and the Canaanite woman is a great one: that we are important and that persistence is powerful. As we work, sometimes against all "rational" voices, to bring something better into existence, let us remember this story and know that if what we are asking will ultimately serve the will of God, it will be granted. Prayer *is* answered. Remember the Magdalene and this woman of Canaan. Dry your tears and persevere.

The Widow and the Significance of Nearly Nothing

Do you ever feel insignificant? I certainly do. After all, who are we and what effect do we have on the world? We aren't national leaders, church leaders, famous movers and shakers or financiers. We aren't even soap opera stars or talk show guests. We probably aren't the best, the brightest, the most talented or even the most immaculate housekeeper in our circle of friends.

Perhaps we sing in the choir or write letters to the editor or contribute to the bake sale. We may even give talks to local women's clubs or perhaps we're recognized among our intimates as gifted or talented. But neither Washington, D.C. nor Hollywood is beckoning. So what's the point? How can we—the nearly anonymous majority of women—make any difference in the coming of the reign of God? Does anybody even notice...or care?

"He looked up and saw rich people putting their gifts into the treasury; he also saw a poor widow put in two small copper coins. He said, 'Truly I tell you, this poor widow has put in more than all of them; for all of them have contributed out of their abundance, but she out of her poverty has put in all she had to live on'" (Lk 21:1-4).

Could it be that our answers lie there? Could it be that God recognizes and blesses our "little" gifts and talents, our small generosities? Yes, and yes again.

In this story, Jesus tells us that we are not judged against one another. Rather, our challenge lies in ourselves. What God wants is our personal best, whatever that might be and however it might be expressed.

We are healed in knowing that what we give in the service of God is enough, as long as it is our all. Perhaps our contribution will never be more than the best chocolate cake at the church bake sale. In the eyes of Jesus, if we have put all our love and caring into baking that cake, it is of infinitely greater value than a casual donation of a dozen cakes from a large bakery.

On those days when we are feeling particularly unimportant, we need only think of the poor widow at the treasury. We don't have to be the best at anything except at being ourselves. That is all God asks from us and it is within our power to say our "yes" and to live it.

The Others

Think of Jesus and the many women he helped: the adulteress whom he refused to regard as a sinful object, but in whom he saw the potential of her humanity and blessed it (cf. Jn 8:3-11); Peter's mother-in-law, ill with a fever, whom Jesus healed in order that she might be able to serve (cf. Mt 8:14-15); the widow of Naim and her grief, healed by Jesus (cf. Lk 7:1-17); the women, along with the five thousand men, whom Jesus fed and so healed their hunger (cf. Mk 6:34-44); the bride at Cana whom Jesus could not disappoint (cf. Jn 2:1-11); the women of Jerusalem whom Jesus met as he carried his cross (cf. Lk 23:27-29). We are led to think of the countless other women who heard him speak, who brushed against him in crowds, who walked with him on the dusty roads of Galilee.

Then let us think of the crippled woman in the synagogue...and laugh!

The Crippled Woman

"Now he was teaching in one of the synagogues on the sabbath. And just then there appeared a woman with a spirit that had crippled her for eighteen years. She was bent over and was quite unable to stand up straight. When Jesus saw her, he called her over and said, 'Woman, you are set free from your ailment.' When he laid his hands on her, immediately she stood up straight and began praising God" (Lk 13:10-13).

Does Jesus want women to stand up straight, to be healed? Yes. Is Jesus against any spirit that keeps us bent and in subjection? Yes. Does Jesus eagerly lay hands on us even before we ask? Yes.

As the Father created us whole and beautiful, so the Son heals what has gone awry that we may be whole and beautiful again. Father and Son breathe out the Spirit, who brings us into the fullness of our womanhood. Let us remember the gift, stand straight and proud in that womanhood, and give glory to God!

Prayer

Jesus, I thank you yet again for your message of love and healing. I thank you for the Canaanite woman's persistence and the widow's mite and for Peter's mother-in-law and all the rest. I thank you for showing us in so many ways the blessing it is to be a woman healed by your compassion.

Please help me to be in touch with whatever in me needs healing. Help me to confront what is wounded or diseased and, in your love, let me be made well. Let me see myself as you see me and help me to live in that new vision. I ask for healing. I know that you will answer me.

I want to be freed of the evil spirit that tells me that woman is something less, that spirit that keeps me bent over and crippled. Lord, fill me instead with your Holy Spirit. Make me straight and strong that I may stand before all the people and give glory to you.

All you women of the Gospel, named and unnamed, pray for all women of this time that we may be healed. Amen.

Jesus Is Waiting for You

This book is not the last word by any stretch of the imagination. Despite my own ego's urge to have the last word, I know that the only truly healing last word is the Word who took on human flesh and came among us, who is still among us, who will be among us.

My hope and prayer for what I have written is that it will encourage you to search the scriptures for yourself and to get to know all the women who live in those pages. Discover their healings and so find your own. Wear out your Bible. You can always get a new one. Or you can bandage up your old one to commemorate the healing you have found there.

The first edition of this book ended with the Beatitudes. At that time, they seemed most fitting. But in the intervening years my own healing has continued and made me even more joyful to be the woman God creates, Jesus redeems, and the Spirit graces. So I want to end a bit differently this time with a Scripture passage that seems to capture in a few words my prayer for all of us.

> Sing aloud, O daughter Zion; shout, O Israel! Rejoice and exult with all your heart, O daughter Jerusalem!

> The Lord has taken away the judgments against you, he has turned away your enemies. The king of Israel, the Lord, is in your midst; you shall fear disaster no more.

The Lord, your God, is in your midst, a warrior who gives victory; he will rejoice over you with gladness, he will renew you in his love; he will exult over you with loud singing as on a day of festival. I will remove disaster from you, so that you will not bear reproach for it (Zeph 3:14-15, 17-18).

Shout for joy, daughter of Zion!
Go in peace.

About the Author

Sister Ruthann Williams, O.P., is a member of the Dominican Sisters of Caldwell, New Jersey. She holds a Master's Degree from Drew University and a second Master's from Immaculate Conception Seminary, Seton Hall University.

In the last several years Sister has given retreats and days of recollection in New Jersey, New York, Pennsylvania, Massachusetts, California, Florida, Maine, Texas, Illinois and Virginia. She has led pilgrimages to Israel and to Medugorje in the former Yugoslavia. Sister has an active women's ministry and leads many days of healing just for women. In the spring of 1992 she organized and directed a national conference for women called "Go In Peace"; in 1993, a second one called "Blessed Are You"; and in 1994, a third titled "Full of Grace"; a fourth in 1995, "Shout for Joy, Daughter of Zion"; and in 1996 a fifth entitled "In the Beginning."

Her articles and poems have been published in regional and national magazines, most recently in *The Priest;*

Brothers, Sisters Today; and *Ruah.* An article which she wrote on pastoral care for the sexually addicted has been translated into several languages for worldwide distribution.

Sister's first book *Healing Your Grief* was published in 1987; her second, the first edition of *Go in Peace: Healing For Women,* in 1990. *Thank You For Hearing My Call,* which Sister co-authored, was also published in 1990. In 1992 a small volume of her poetry, *Mystery,* was released. Sister also has three video tapes in distribution and dozens of audio cassettes.

In June 1991 Sister was honored for her "Outstanding Work in Healing and Evangelization" at the national conference *Healed by Love.* In June 1992 she was again honored, this time for her pioneer work in women's ministry, at a ceremony at Sacred Heart Cathedral in the Archdiocese of Newark, New Jersey.

Sister Ruthann is a member of the Association of Christian Therapists, the National Christian Counselors Association, and the Order of St. Luke.

auline BOOKS & MEDIA

ALASKA
750 West 5th Ave., Anchorage, AK 99501; 907-272-8183

CALIFORNIA
3908 Sepulveda Blvd., Culver City, CA 90230; 310-397-8676
5945 Balboa Ave., San Diego, CA 92111; 619-565-9181
46 Geary Street, San Francisco, CA 94108; 415-781-5180

FLORIDA
145 S.W. 107th Ave., Miami, FL 33174; 305-559-6715

HAWAII
1143 Bishop Street, Honolulu, HI 96813; 808-521-2731

ILLINOIS
172 North Michigan Ave., Chicago, IL 60601; 312-346-4228

LOUISIANA
4403 Veterans Memorial Blvd., Metairie, LA 70006; 504-887-7631

MASSACHUSETTS
50 St. Paul's Ave., Jamaica Plain, Boston, MA 02130; 617-522-8911
Rte. 1, 885 Providence Hwy., Dedham, MA 02026; 617-326-5385

MISSOURI
9804 Watson Rd., St. Louis, MO 63126; 314-965-3512

NEW JERSEY
561 U.S. Route 1, Wick Plaza, Edison, NJ 08817; 908-572-1200

NEW YORK
150 East 52nd Street, New York, NY 10022; 212-754-1110
78 Fort Place, Staten Island, NY 10301; 718-447-5071

OHIO
2105 Ontario Street, Cleveland, OH 44115; 216-621-9427

PENNSYLVANIA
Northeast Shopping Center, 9171-A Roosevelt Blvd., Philadelphia, PA
19114; 215-676-9494

SOUTH CAROLINA
243 King Street, Charleston, SC 29401; 803-577-0175

TENNESSEE
4811 Poplar Ave., Memphis, TN 38117; 901-761-2987

TEXAS
114 Main Plaza, San Antonio, TX 78205; 210-224-8101

VIRGINIA
1025 King Street, Alexandria, VA 22314; 703-549-3806

CANADA
3022 Dufferin Street, Toronto, Ontario, Canada M6B 3T5; 416-781-9131